Project Management in Libraries, Archives and Museums

Chandos
Information Professional Series

Series Editor: Ruth Rikowski
(email: Rikowskigr@aol.com)

Chandos' new series of books are aimed at the busy information professional. They have been specially commissioned to provide the reader with an authoritative view of current thinking. They are designed to provide easy-to-read and (most importantly) practical coverage of topics that are of interest to librarians and other information professionals. If you would like a full listing of current and forthcoming titles, please visit our website www.chandospublishing.com or email info@chandospublishing.com or telephone +44 (0) 1223 891358.

New authors: we are always pleased to receive ideas for new titles; if you would like to write a book for Chandos, please contact Dr Glyn Jones on email gjones@chandospublishing.com or telephone number +44 (0) 1993 848726.

Bulk orders: some organisations buy a number of copies of our books. If you are interested in doing this, we would be pleased to discuss a discount.
Please email info@chandospublishing.com or telephone +44 (0) 1223 891358.

Project Management in Libraries, Archives and Museums

Working with government and other external partners

Julie Carpenter

Oxford Cambridge New Delhi

Chandos Publishing
TBAC Business Centre
Avenue 4
Station Lane
Witney
Oxford OX28 4BN
UK
Tel: +44 (0) 1993 848726
Email: info@chandospublishing.com
www.chandospublishing.com

Chandos Publishing is an imprint of Woodhead Publishing Limited

Woodhead Publishing Limited
80 High Street
Sawston
Cambridge CB22 3HJ
UK
Tel: +44 (0) 1223 499140
Fax: +44 (0) 1223 832819
www.woodheadpublishing.com

First published in 2011

ISBN:
978 1 84334 566 4

British Library Cataloguing-in-Publication Data.
A catalogue record for this book is available from the British Library.

Typeset by RefineCatch Limited, Bungay, Suffolk
Printed in the UK and USA.

Contents

List of figures and tables

Figures

Tables

Acknowledgements

Like my first book, *Library Project Funding: A guide to writing and planning proposals* (Chandos), this book draws upon a wide range of sources from a variety of different sectors. Some of these are published sources which I have tried and tested in a number of professional project and training situations; others are materials I have discovered during the course of writing this book, many of them web-only resources which are likely to evolve and change, and it is inevitable that some of the web links will fail over time. All of the sources are referenced and acknowledged in the text if I have quoted or adapted excerpts from them and resources that I consider to be particularly valuable are also described more fully in the final section on useful resources.

My thanks go to the authors and project management experts who have made their expertise available, many of whom are from completely different professional backgrounds and sectors than ours, and whose work I have tried to make accessible and relevant here to colleagues in the cultural heritage and academic sectors.

List of abbreviations and acronyms

CPA	critical path analysis
DFID	Department for International Development (UK)
EU	European Union
fEC	full economic costing
ICT	information and communication technology
JISC	Joint Information Systems Committee of the UK Higher Education Funding Councils
LSP	Local Strategic Partnership
M&E	monitoring and evaluation
MSC	most significant change
PCM	project cycle management
PERT	programme evaluation and review technique
PME	project monitoring and evaluation
QMS	quality management system
RFP	request for proposal
SROI	social return on investment
TRAC	transparent approach to costing
UAT	user acceptance test
UFE	utilisation-focused evaluation
UNESCO	United Nations Educational, Scientific and Cultural Organization

About the author

Julie Carpenter is a qualified librarian and director of the independent consulting, research and project management company, Education for Change Ltd (*http://www.efc.co.uk*).

She left the British Council in 1990 after 12 years of working all over the world, with a latter focus on book and information sector review and policy development in the education sector, working with DFID, the World Bank and the UK Publishers Association in several African and Asian countries. She continued information services policy review and management work for DFID, UNESCO, UNIDO, the World Bank and other international development agencies in Eastern Europe, in China, Korea, Iran and the Caribbean. By the mid-1990s she had successfully initiated and developed two multinational research projects for the European Commission's Telematics for Libraries Programme and became the Project Manager of the project MOBILE (1994–7) with research partner institutions in three EU states.

From 1996 to 1998 she worked with the Asian Development Bank, providing technical assistance in project preparation and consulting services for the first Mongolia Education Sector Development Project. In 1997, she became the Scheme Administrator and Project Manager for DFID's *British Books for Managers* scheme (1997–2001), developing a book subsidy and translation support programme for the newly privatised book trade and publishers in 19 Central and Eastern European countries.

More recently she has been working on research and consulting contracts in the UK, with academic and cultural heritage institutions focusing on the impact of electronic information services and digitisation of collections. With colleagues in Education for Change she manages a range of multi-stakeholder and frequently multi-country projects in education and other social sectors.

The author may be contacted via the publishers.

1

What does project management mean?

Introduction

Projects are a common feature in the work of libraries, archives and museums. They may be activities which are part of a broader programme of strategic change, or externally-funded initiatives perceived as somehow 'separate' from operational realities.

The 'projectisation' of work has led to the widespread use of 'project' terminology: people talk about 'project managing' something, when they often mean problem-solving and decision-making; IT 'projects' can mean anything from the introduction across an institution of some new application, to a full-scale system procurement; things tend to be 'implemented' rather than 'executed' or simply 'done'; institutions might adopt a 'project-approach' to management issues. The word 'project' itself is so widely used in so many different contexts that its meaning has become rather vague.

This first chapter will explore the most common approaches to project management and to the main roles and responsibilities of a project manager.

What is a project?

So what do we mean by a project? Most definitions emphasise the following common features of projects:

- They are temporary – that is, they have definite start and end dates; when the work is complete the project is finished and remaining resources may be dispersed.
- They have definable aims, objectives and outcomes, which almost always involve something unique, some innovation or change, with results that are different from other day-to-day functions or outputs of the organisation.
- They use defined and predetermined resources to achieve the required outcomes.

The PRINCE2 methodology takes a process-driven approach and the project is seen as the structures and resources set up to deliver something. In the service-driven world of libraries, museums and archives, however, people are more inclined to think of projects as the development and delivery of the outcomes of those structures and resources – an important difference, in my view, with implications for the way projects might be managed.

Of course, each project falls within a specific business context and there will be many high-level and strategic issues and circumstances surrounding a project, which will be the concern of senior organisational managers, and possibly parent bodies. The project manager often sits in the middle ground between higher-level more strategic concerns that provide context, and the specialist techniques and resources that are required to achieve the project's aims.

Kinds of projects

Sheila Corrall[1] defines three broad types of projects as types of activities with different degrees of frequency and impact:

- Runners – 'bread and butter' undertakings that occur quite frequently, and rarely present major challenges as the organisation is well set up to deal with them;
- Repeaters – 'out-of-the-ordinary' undertakings, that happen less often and represent enough variation to require significantly more attention;
- Strangers – 'one-off' undertakings, where the organisation has little or no past experience, involving many interests and functions.

Barbara Allan[2] also identifies a category of projects as 'strategic or operational' and explores the levels of complexity in a project, making the useful point that:

> The more complex the project then the more important it is to use project management tools and techniques – these are the types of projects they were designed to support. In contrast, using these tools and techniques on relatively simple projects is rather like using a sledgehammer to crack a nut.

Table 1.1 adapts Allan's summary of the key differences between simple and complex projects.

This book focuses in particular on managing projects which involve a range of internal and external partners, which adds an inevitable level of complexity no matter how relatively simple are the aims and objectives, or how low the levels of innovation.

Table 1.1 **Simple and complex projects**

Characteristics	Relatively simple projects	Complex projects
	e.g. moving office, creating a new website, or organising a conference	e.g. national digitisation project, merging two archives, implementing a new institutional repository
People	Involvement of a small group of people who are all working in the same building and organisation	Involvement of people from different professional backgrounds, different teams and organisations. Involvement of people with a range of first languages, from different cultures, or living in different time zones. Involvement of a large number of different activities involving a number of different people
Data	Relatively low volumes of data	Involves large volumes of data
Risks	Risks can be easily identified	Hard to identify all the risks
Innovation	Low levels of innovation; while the project may be novel to the project team there is existing good practice in this type of work	High levels of innovation
Technology	Working with relatively well-established and tested technology	Working in a technical environment that is changing at a rapid pace; working with technologies that are new to the local environment and not well-supported

Working methods	Use of tried and tested methods (even if they are new to the project team)	Working procedures are established by an external body which may change them throughout the project
Management	Project manager has complete control over the project	External body or another person may have real power e.g. over timescale, resources, people. Responsibility for the project may be shared e.g. by managers working in different organisations
Environment	Well known to project workers. Little change in the environment over the lifetime of the project	Turbulent with constant change caused by business environment, government or other external factors

Project or programme

Programme management is the process of managing several related projects, often with specific organisational change or performance enhancement goals. The programme can be the overall organisational plan within a policy framework, which sets the overall outcome and budget limits, defines the geographical, social and economic parameters within which the programme operates, and will be established for a number of years.

The project is a set of activities designed to achieve a stated objective, based on an identified problem within the parameters of the programme, which links the higher level policy initiative of the programme with the problems faced by a particular group at service and operational levels.

A programme is often described as a 'portfolio' of projects (for instance, in UK higher education), designed to exploit economies of scale and to reduce coordination costs and risks. The project manager's job is to ensure that their project succeeds, while the programme manager may not care much about individual projects but is concerned with the cumulative results or ultimate goals.

Programme management may focus on selecting the best group of projects, defining them in terms of their objectives and providing an environment where projects can be run successfully. In the UK a good example of programme management is the Joint Information Systems Committee (JISC) of the Higher Education Funding Councils, which provides funds under a number of different programmes to support UK colleges and universities 'in the innovative use of digital technologies, helping to maintain the UK's position as a global leader in education'. These programmes are managed by the JISC and the funds are invested in a range of projects relevant to each programme's goals, which are managed and delivered by colleges, universities and other stakeholders in the academic sector.[3]

Project and programme management are complementary and related disciplines: this book is concerned primarily with project management, though pointers to useful guidance on programme or portfolio management are included in the final section on useful resources.

The project lifecycle approach to project management

It is common, particularly in international development funding contexts, to describe the processes involved in project management as a project cycle, moving through project identification or initiation, design, implementation and evaluation. There are many variations on the project cycle (see examples below) all with basically the same purpose of formalising what otherwise might seem unstructured activities, undertaken outside the everyday operations of organisations and with multiple stakeholders. For instance, the European Commission guidelines for EuropeAid tell us:

> The way in which projects are planned and carried out follows a sequence beginning with an agreed strategy, which leads to an idea for a specific action, oriented towards achieving a set of objectives, which then is formulated, implemented, and evaluated with a view to improving the strategy and further action. The project cycle provides a structure to ensure that stakeholders are consulted and relevant information is available, so that informed decisions can be made at key stages in the life of a project.[4]

The project cycle is frequently illustrated diagrammatically, showing how each 'stage' in the cycle feeds into the next stage, and indicating the iterative nature of some of the activities, such as evaluation and identification. Figure 1.1 and Figure 1.2 are examples.

Figure 1.1 **The project cycle for EuropeAid**

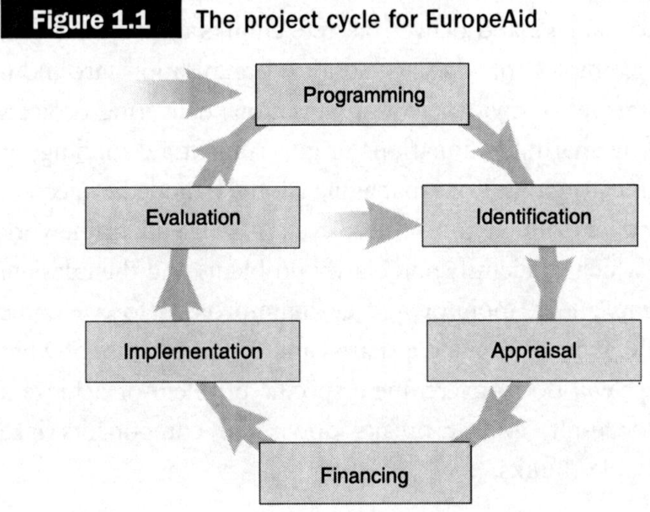

Figure 1.2 **The project cycle from Tearfund**[5]

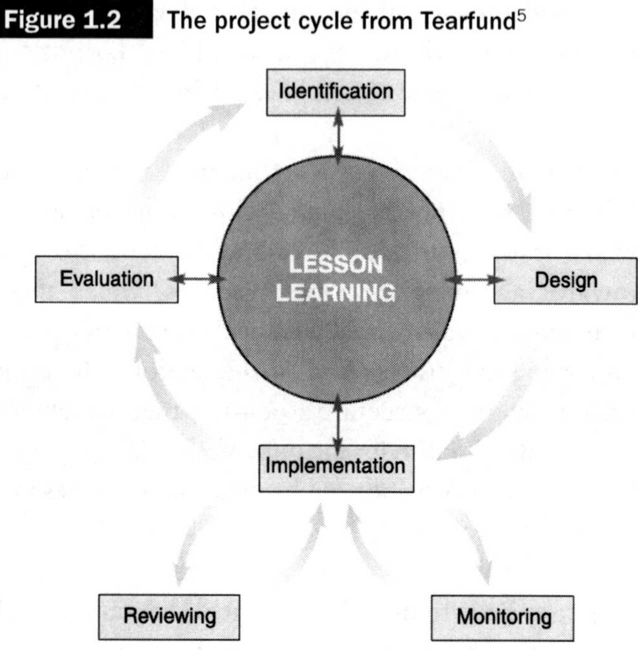

The project cycle management (PCM) approach is particularly relevant, in my view, for organisations that 'live by projects' – that is, their operations are funded on an almost entirely project-funding basis, albeit from different funders, and the organisation exists to manage and deliver discrete chunks of project work. Good examples of these kinds of organisation are non-governmental or civil society organisations delivering projects funded by charitable donations or government aid funding; or community organisations managing a lottery-funded project. In this kind of context the project cycle is a useful framework within which to identify and clarify problems and then design, plan, implement, monitor and evaluate projects to overcome them. PCM helps to build a shared and concise picture of what a project will do to overcome a specific problem or achieve a required result, and it breaks down the components into manageable chunks.

As Freer Spreckley tells us:

> PCM provides the context in which project decisions are made and activities managed: it maintains the critical linkage between one stage and the next. As a common methodology PCM also provides the basis for a partnership framework when more than one agency is engaged in planning or managing projects. An organisation that uses PCM will have to adjust their operational procedures and working style to fully benefit from the methodology.[6]

And herein lies the main problem I have with the project cycle approach to project management: it is just not a realistic proposition to change operational procedures and working styles within most libraries, museums and archives to meet the requirements of projects that are likely to represent only a fraction of the overall value and spend of the organisation. Projects that are being planned, managed and implemented within the context of a service delivery organisation (that is itself almost certainly a smaller component of a much larger, publicly funded institution) need to be integrated within wider operational procedures and strategic objectives, perhaps even transferring into service elements at project end. They may look and feel just like the 'core business' of their organisation, being projects only in the sense that they rely on limited external or special funding. The use of PCM methods in these contexts could be detrimental to the project's credibility and sustainability.

Moreover, the experience of project management rarely reflects a clear progression from one stage in the project cycle to the next: even implementation can start on one part of a project while some other activities may still be in the planning stage, and funding for yet other planned activities may not be secured until after the project starts. These are the realities of blending project work with ongoing service operation and delivery in libraries, archives and museums, with core budgets supplemented by often very considerable project funding for innovation, regeneration or development.

PRINCE2

PRINCE2 recognises the need for the integration of project management processes into corporate operations while maintaining standards of accountability, efficiency and effectiveness. The PRINCE2 method adopts a process approach to project management, which is undoubtedly of more value to those organisations in which projects are or should be embedded into operations, the processes defining eight distinct management activities to be carried out during a project (see Figure 1.3). Project 'implementation' in PRINCE2 is the management process of 'controlling a

Figure 1.3 PRINCE2 process model

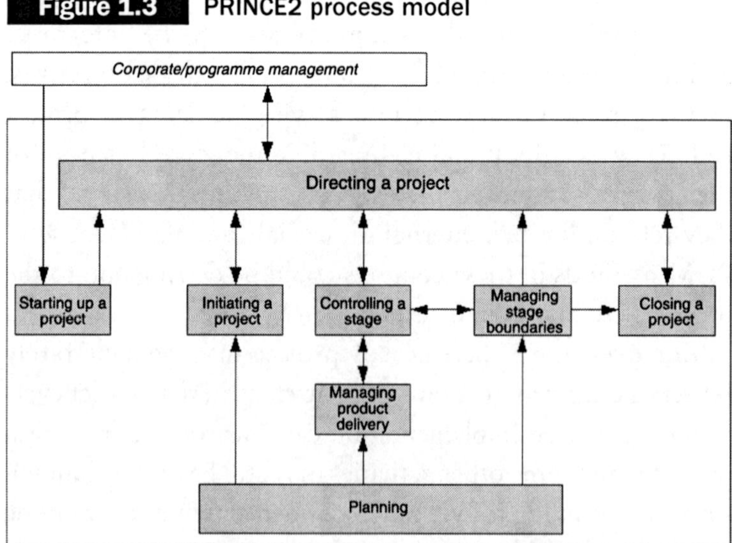

stage', perhaps mediated by 'quality review', leading to 'managing product delivery', with 'no attempt . . . made to lay out the steps in a strict sequence, since such a hard and fast sequence seldom exists'.[7]

In addition, PRINCE2 specifies a number of 'components' that are specific management approaches that should be applied within these activities or processes as appropriate: these components include:

- business case development;
- organisation and management structure of the project team;
- planning at different levels;
- controls including review and decision-making procedures;
- management of risk;
- quality in a project environment.

Although this book does not suggest the wholesale adoption of PRINCE2 methodology, it draws on its approaches where they can be seen to be applicable to a cultural heritage or library and information service context. It is important for project managers within libraries, museums and archives to be aware of the basic elements of PRINCE2, since it is widely used in both the public and private sectors, and is frequently adopted as a methodology in local and central government. Originally developed for the needs of IT projects, the method has also been used on many non-IT projects and in 2009 the latest version was explicitly designed to make the method simpler and 'lighter'.

Why project management – why projects fail

In theory, project management is a set of methods used to initiate, plan, organise and manage the project through to completion. As a real world experience it is really the marshalling of a range of management skills and techniques within a project rather than an operational situation: that is, drawing together and employing a disparate range of predetermined resources, to achieve a set of defined objectives and outcomes, within a strictly defined timescale. The PRINCE2 handbook points out that a project manager should manage by exception, that is, a project plan is agreed at the highest level appropriate and then the project manager gets on with it unless something is forecast to go wrong.

In order to understand the nature of project management, it is useful to consider some of the reasons why projects can fail: for instance:

- insufficient attention to checking that a valid business case exists;
- insufficient attention to quality at the outset and during development;
- insufficient definition of the required outcomes, leading to confusion over what the project is expected to achieve;
- lack of communication with stakeholders and interested parties, leading to products being delivered that are not what the customer wanted;
- inadequate planning and coordination of resources;
- insufficient or lack of measurable control over progress, so that projects do not reveal their exact status until too late.[8]

These are clearly management deficiencies, due to ineffective project management or 'the wrong project manager, i.e. someone without the necessary project management, motivational, leadership and change agent skills'.[9] It is too often true, particularly in service sector organisations, that a major reason for project failure is lack of appreciation at high levels within the organisation of the importance of project management, or the inadequate definition of the project manager's role and responsibilities leading to lack of direction and poor decision-making.

Project management role and responsibilities

The traditional process-driven project management role is focused around a project life cycle which typically follows these stages:

- project initiation;
- planning the project process;
- implementing the project;
- evaluating and reviewing the project;
- disseminating information about the project and its outcomes.

Table 1.2 presents a more management-oriented perspective on the role and main responsibilities of a typical project manager.

PRINCE2 notes that the project manager's role is to manage the work, not to do it, and 'it may be beneficial to employ high-quality people part time rather than lesser quality people full time' in the project manager role. The many different aspects of the role are illustrated in Figure 1.4.

Barbara Allan[10] emphasises the importance of adopting a people-centred approach to project management as it is likely to motivate both the project team and other stakeholders to ensure that the project is successful. I would endorse this view particularly in the academic and cultural heritage

Table 1.2 **A view of project management roles and responsibilities**

Issues	Typical steps
1. Planning and resource allocation	■ Review existing project plans and proposed resources ■ Development/refinement of robust business case ■ Define and source appropriate resources (including securing funding) ■ Develop project partnership and decision-making structures
2. Quality control (processes and outputs)	■ Define what type of information needs to be collected, how it should be systematised and stored ■ Define when monitoring activities should take place ■ Define how to use and present monitoring results, conclusions and recommendations ■ Plan for evaluations involving a wider range of stakeholders
3. Information, communication and reporting	■ Define whom to inform about decisions and their implications for budgets, resource allocation, activity re-scheduling etc. ■ Define what is necessary in terms of formal communications; when, to whom and in which form the information should be made available
4. Financial planning	■ Forecast financial resources over time, to the level of detail required and when ■ Determine when to review expenditure and to adjust forecasts to ensure availability of funds when required
5. Staff/personnel management	■ Define tasks, roles and responsibilities of project personnel (including external contributors) ■ Identify training needs to perform tasks and organise required training ■ Ensure team building and motivation of staff

Figure 1.4 PRINCE2: the many facets of the project manager role

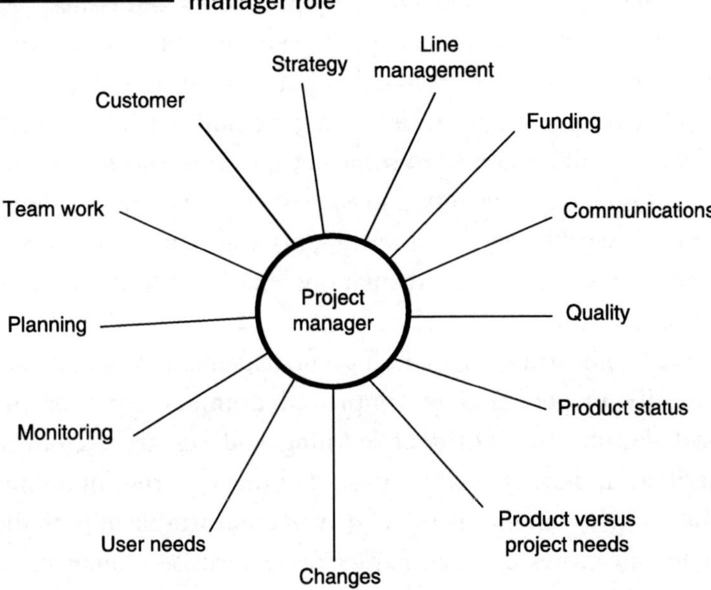

sectors where the principal resource and main costs are the project personnel, and where partnerships across large organisations and with external partners are often of paramount importance. It could be said within these sectors that the main role of the project manager is not only about getting things done on time, but is about getting them done within a context of participative decision-making: acting effectively to facilitate others to get involved, make decisions and take responsibility.

Projects management in libraries, museums and archives

This particular emphasis on human resources is one of several distinguishing characteristics of libraries, museums and archives, which needs to be taken into account when considering project management approaches and issues.

These are overwhelmingly public service organisations, very often embedded within parent bodies, such as universities, local government authorities, and government agencies, each of which will be subject to some key government policies and operational requirements, and each of which will have its own strategic world view and priorities, management structure and ethos, procedures and regulations that will impact upon projects.

Although strategic planning, management practice and capacity in general have improved dramatically over the past decade, the world of learning and research, cultural heritage and artistic exploration that our libraries, museums and archives inhabit is still a fairly uncomfortable fit with the style and mores of customer-driven enterprise management or product-driven manufacturing. While it may be likely that the senior managers of services and local government authority departments are expert and comfortable with PRINCE2 project management approaches and methods, most project managers within libraries, museums and archives are more likely to come from middle management grades and have professional or curatorial rather than management backgrounds. Project management skills and practices need to grow organically from the professional knowledge and experience of these practitioners, so that they feel like a good fit with the service ethos most common to our organisations, rather than a set of skills imported from another world and bolted on to an existing portfolio.

Projects of one sort or another are part of virtually every practitioner's life these days. Project management needs to be demystified and developed to fit organisational cultures and realities.

What does this book do?

This book adopts a pragmatic approach to project management, following the lead of PRINCE2 and focusing on the main management activities and management concerns that have to be used and addressed at various (and often multiple) points in the life of a project. Table 1.3 illustrates this by relating these main activities to a 'project cycle' view:

Table 1.3 Management activities (processes)

Typical project cycle stages	Planning and review	Managing partnerships	Managing risk	Managing resources	Managing monitoring and evaluation
Identification/ design	X	X	X	X	
Appraisal/ financing	X		X		X
Implementation	X	X	X	X	X
Evaluation/ lesson learning	X				X

The starting point of all project management roles is the project plans. They may have been developed as a project proposal or as part of a strategic planning exercise by someone other than the designated project manager and quite some time may have passed since the initial planning exercise. Review, revision and monitoring of these plans are the subject of Chapter 2.

Chapter 3 looks at managing project partnerships, including the challenges of working across different sectors and types of organisation, governance and management structures, partner roles and responsibilities, reporting and accountability.

Partnerships are a source of potential risks in projects, and these need to be managed within the project partnership structures: Chapter 4 considers these and other risks and techniques for identifying and managing them.

Since most projects within the library and cultural heritage sector are labour-intensive and people-oriented, managing teams, and monitoring and managing effort and time, play a large part in project management processes. This is the focus of Chapter 5.

Equally importantly, Chapter 6 focuses on the monitoring and management of other project resources – time, money and externally sourced goods and services. The chapter returns to the first planning phases, where understanding and working with specific procedures, such as the government's transparent approach to costing (TRAC) and full economic costing (fEC), can have a dramatic effect on project management.

All projects will need periodic evaluation and review, and Chapter 7 considers evaluation methodologies, how to specify and commission evaluations, reviews and impact assessments.

Chapter 8 looks at quality management in projects, demystifying some of the critical quality issues and terminology that arise in quality management systems often adopted by parent bodies.

Chapter 9 considers the related issue of ensuring sustainability of project outcomes, whether transferring a project into practice within wider service delivery or pursuing revenue generation strategies.

Much is made of ICT-based tools and applications for project management: Chapter 10 considers the uses of MS Project, the MS Office suite, and open source alternatives, as well as more generic web-based tools in a project management context.

The book concludes with a section on web-based and other resources that the author has found useful and a glossary of common project management terms.

Notes

1. Sheila Corrall. *Strategic Management of Information Services: A Planning Handbook*. London: Aslib/IMI, 2000.
2. Barbara Allan. *Project Management: Tools and Techniques for Today's ILS Professional*. London: Facet, 2004.
3. See *http://www.jisc.ac.uk/whatwedo/programmes.aspx*.
4. European Commission (2002) *EuropeAid Co-operation Office General Affairs Evaluation. Project Cycle Management Handbook. Version 2.0 March 2002*. Prepared by PARTICIP GmbH.
5. Rachel Blackman. *Project Cycle Management*, Roots Resources 5. London: Tearfund, 2003.
6. Freer Spreckley. *Project Cycle Management Toolkit*, 3rd edn. Local Livelihoods Ltd, 2006. Online at: *http://www.locallivelihoods.com*.
7. *Managing Successful Projects with PRINCE2*. London: TSO, 2005.
8. Ibid.
9. Allan, op. cit.
10. Ibid.

2

Project planning and review

Introduction

Although this book makes the assumption that a project plan has already been developed, this chapter considers the critical elements of project planning. Planning and re-planning are part of project management that have to be done at regular intervals. Project work plans and schedules are important management tools. In the PRINCE2 methodology planning is a repeatable process and plays an important role in other project management processes.

Project initiation

In the first instance, however, with the project approved in principle, PRINCE2 recommends a period of project initiation, which includes a detailed review of existing project plans and the project business case to ensure that the investment of time and effort required is justified; to enable and encourage the project board or appropriate management to take ownership of the project; and to provide the baseline for decision-making processes. This approach is similar in scope and purpose to a typical Inception Period or Phase in a project.

Project implementation begins with the inception period often covering a period of several months during which project organisation including administrative, financial and technical responsibilities are set up, and the initial planning of the appraisal phase is updated and refined. The mechanisms and tools developed for this purpose are then used throughout the following periods of implementation. The inception period usually consists of the following elements:

- set-up of the project office and staff recruitment;
- if required, implementation of a study to update baseline information;
- discussions with major stakeholders, if possible including target groups, to complete and update the Logical Framework, to prepare the Overall Work Plan and the Activity and Resource Schedules. (Ideally, this should be done in a participatory workshop session . . . depending on the complexity of the project);
- preparation and submission of the Overall Work Plan (incorporating the project's internal Monitoring and Evaluation Plan).[1]

Revisiting the project plan

At the start of a project the overall status of the project plan may be questionable – is it still accurate; does it still reflect organisational realities; is it detailed enough to begin its implementation? For instance, the following situations may be familiar in library, museum and archive projects:

- The project proposal and plan were developed as a funding proposal by a member of staff who has since moved on, and does not include a detailed work plan or business case.
- The project proposal and plan were submitted for funding approval in a previous financial year, since when various changes in organisational structures and budgets have taken place.
- The designated project manager was not involved in the original round of project proposal preparation and planning, and the rationale and assumptions made as part of that process are not clearly defined.
- Funding has been awarded for a series of identified projects on the basis of a programme level business plan involving several partners, and individual detailed project plans have not been developed although work on the programme has already commenced.

An effective project plan should become a working document, kept under review and updated in response to change. It follows that, in these kinds of circumstances, the first task of the project manager must be to undertake a detailed review and possibly revision of the project plan. This may involve renegotiating certain aspects of it, and reassessing what can be achieved with the allocated budget in changed circumstances.

The essential characteristics of a project can be summarised as a plane triangle (see Figure 2.1) in which the angles represent cost, time and performance, circumscribed by regulatory or external constraints. As with any triangle, you cannot change one angle without affecting one or both the others. For instance, the time schedule of your project cannot be changed without affecting either cost or performance or

Figure 2.1 **The essential characteristics of a project**

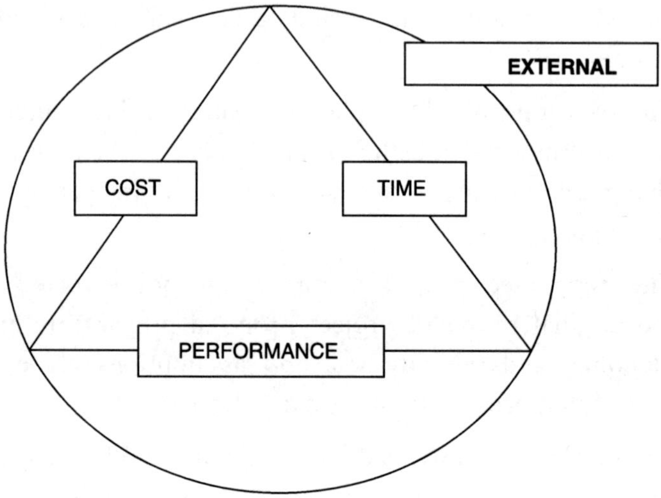

both. Projects are always planned and implemented against a background of risk as well as external constraints.

Whether designed for an externally funded project or for a project within an internally driven programme of organisational change the project plan will include a detailed work plan with the following elements:

- Defined work content or work packages, tasks and activities, with specific targets representing the actions and actual deliverables required within the project timescale in order to fulfil the objectives and achieve the project aims.
- Specified staff and responsibilities related to specific work packages, with calculated duration, effort and elapsed time, ensuring that the project work plan can be delivered effectively and on time.
- A time schedule for the work based on these calculations.

Project planning activities

The main planning activities involved in developing, reviewing and potentially revising a project plan should ideally be done by the project manager and the project team, so that work content and responsibilities can be reviewed from a number of different perspectives and the resulting work plan will be more robust and reliable.

Project planning can be broken down into the following activities:

- review of the project aims, purpose, objectives and required outcomes;
- analysis of the work content into work packages, tasks and activities;
- consideration of effort and duration of each task and of elapsed time;
- determination of the logical sequence for each work package, its prerequisites and outcomes (scheduling);
- construction of a project timetable based on the above;
- consideration of the resources required to complete each work package and their costs.

Reviewing the project objectives

Project objectives need to be SMART:

Specific – in terms of desired results and responsibility for delivery

Measurable – either quantitatively or by demonstrating qualitative achievement

Acceptable – to stakeholders (ideally agreed with and owned by them)

Realistic – in relation to environmental factors and available resources

Time-bound – according to the particular project context

They also need to make sense within existing policy and operational contexts. The key issue to consider, when reviewing project objectives, is whether it is clear what the critical success factor or factors will be for each one – in other words, what *outcomes* must be manifest at the end of the project for it to be considered a success.

In each project there is likely to be a range of success factors or outcomes, some of which will be essential and some merely desirable. Deciding on the outcomes and their level of priority provides a measure for project evaluation and also helps to identify the critical tasks in project planning.

Work content and task analysis

Establishing the work content for a project requires the identification of high-level critical tasks or activities required to achieve each objective. This starts from the identified success factors or desirable outcomes that should emerge from the achievement of each objective.

As an example, here are three of the objectives drafted for a European Union project to set up a digital preservation network of library and archival organisations.

1. To identify and raise awareness of sources of information about the preservation of digital objects across the broad spectrum of national and regional cultural and scientific heritage activity in Europe.

2. To appraise and evaluate information sources and documented developments in digital preservation on behalf of Network Members; and to make available results of research, projects, and best practice.
3. To provide an enquiry and advisory service on digital preservation issues, practice, technology and developments.

The success factors or essential outcomes of these objectives could be:

- high-quality information sources relevant to digital preservation across Europe *identified*;
- effective *collection* of peer-reviewed high quality content;
- *provision of effective access* to information and content for target beneficiaries;
- *improved levels of awareness* of European best practice and key issues among target beneficiaries.

To achieve those outcomes the high-level critical tasks, therefore, are likely to include:

- *identification and assembling* of high-quality content and information;
- *presentation of and provision of access* to content and information in user-friendly formats;
- *promotion and dissemination* of assembled content and information to target beneficiaries.

These high-level activities represent the basis for a set of work packages, each with its own sub-objectives, tasks and activities; such as:

Work package 1: Adding content

Work package 2: Technology infrastructure and instruments

Work package 3: Service and product development and delivery

A 'package' of work is a fairly big chunk of a particular kind of activity. 'Adding content', for instance, is activity related to the identification, acquisition and review of information and content from a wide variety of sources and in a variety of formats. Together these work packages will contribute to the achievement of the project's objectives. Work packages are concerned with the operational aspects of the project rather than the aspirational ones. They describe what work needs to be done to put aims and objectives into practice, and to achieve the desired outcomes.

Each work package should have its own sub-objectives, which themselves further break down the overall or broad activity. These in turn should then be further broken down into a set of key tasks or chunks of work. Here, for example, are the main tasks associated with the second of these work packages:

Work package2: Technology infrastructure and instruments

Description of work

Task 1 – Implement the technological infrastructure.

Task 2 – Design web site and templates for local web page creation.

Task 3 – Set up, maintain and publicise web site and Zone-specific pages.

Task 4 – Provide basic training in web page creation etc to Consortium Contractors.

Task 5 – Design and pilot templates for data collection, case studies and other instruments.

Duration and effort

The project plan will specify how long each of the identified work packages, tasks and activities will take (in days, weeks, or months) and how much effort they will require (in person-days, person-weeks, or person-months). Because most projects in service-oriented organisations such as libraries, museums and archives are highly labour-intensive, with people as the main resource, these two concepts of duration and effort are crucial to the effective scheduling of a project and need to be kept constantly under review by the project manager. The basis for calculating them both is the same – how long will the work take to complete? It might take, for instance, one member of staff working alone on a task six days to complete the work: that would be six days in elapsed time and six days of effort. However, if two members of staff are deployed to work together on the same task it should only take three days to complete it – the duration of that task will then have been three days in elapsed time, but still six days in terms of effort.

Calculating duration

Sometimes it is very difficult to estimate duration accurately. Some tasks are unit-based. For instance, there is a known number of books to be catalogued; the time taken for each unit can be measured and multiplied to give the likely duration of the task. Other tasks are activity-based, that is the task is a single unit and it takes as long as it takes. The PERT method of estimating the duration of a task will help with accurate forecasting:

- O – the most optimistic estimate of time
- L – the most likely estimate of time
- P – the most pessimistic estimate

The duration will be (O + [4 × L] + P)/6. So if you think it will probably take 15 days to analyse the replies of a questionnaire, but if you work hard it might take only 8, but on the other hand, if something else crops up it might take 20 – then the likely duration is (8 + [4 × 15] + 20)/6 or 14.6 days.

Estimating effort

If the task in hand is fairly routine and repetitive then devoting more members of staff to it will directly affect how long it will take to complete in elapsed time. However, this may not always be possible with more complex, activity-based tasks: they may be tasks that only one person has the skills to do, and dividing the work up between a number of different people may have an adverse effect on the quality of the work.

It is also likely that several staff, at different levels of seniority (and therefore attracting different costs) will contribute small amounts of time to any one task during its implementation. The project plan should reflect judgements about how much time (in person-days) will be required from staff members at different levels and the total effort required to complete the work package or whole project will be the sum total of all their contributions.

Scheduling

Staging

Staging is usually essential to organise and control more complex projects. A very large project will be planned in

Figure 2.2 **Project structure and schedule for complex projects**

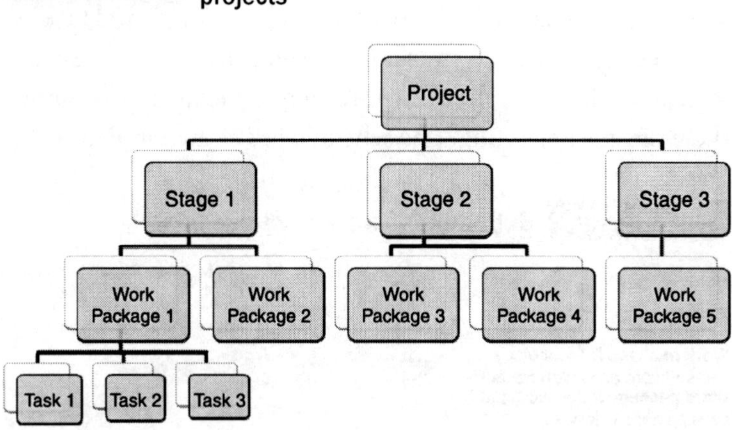

many stages, each of them like mini-projects on their own (see Figure 2.2) – all having to be scheduled so that necessary steps are complete in time for the next stage.

Milestones

Within each project milestones are built in at critical points where there may be a review of progress against the project plan. Milestones are usually significant events or decision points in the project. They are frequently used as payment points by an external funding organisation once a satisfactory progress report or review has been completed. If the project is organised in stages then a milestone would come at the end of each stage. Simple milestone charts, presented in columns showing short verbal descriptions with planned and actual completion dates, provide a useful summary. For multi-dimensional projects, milestones can be depicted as a network of 'results paths' showing dependencies.

Work package and task sequences

The project schedule will order the work packages and tasks so that dependencies and overlap between activities are clear and logical. In the example of the three work packages used above, the work packages might be scheduled as shown in Figure 2.3:

Figure 2.3 Schedule of work packages

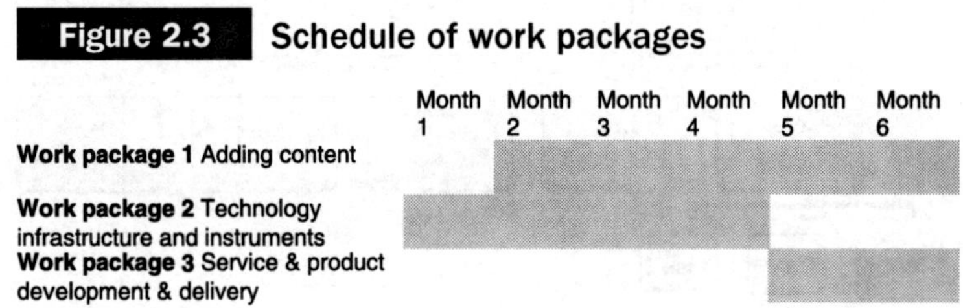

Using critical path analysis (CPA) in project scheduling breaks down a complex task into component activities to optimise performance. Any task involving more than a single operation can be analysed into sets of component activities. Success or failure of the project can result from the management and scheduling of these activities. Information on likely activity durations, costs and logically necessary sequences can be used to optimise project performance.

Some activities depend on others: they can only begin when other activities have been completed. Other activities can take place concurrently. The whole project is only complete when all activities have been completed.

Some activities in the project will be *critical*: if these are delayed at all then the whole project is delayed. Other activities are non-critical: these can be delayed a certain amount without delaying the whole project.

Elapsed time

Some of the work packages and tasks run in parallel and some overlap. Total time from the beginning to end (of a task, work package, stage or whole project) is elapsed time. Delay (or 'slack') is usually deliberately built into a project since it provides useful reflection time and allows flexibility if tasks run over time. 'Lead time' occurs between dependent tasks. If, for example, a man is decorating a room he will need to let the paint dry before he hangs the paper. Overlapping tasks should also have an inbuilt 'lag' – time is required, for instance, for a questionnaire to be returned before analysis of the results can begin.

Timetabling

The project timetable is based on the estimates of elapsed time for work packages and tasks, giving each of these their start and finish dates. This exercise is greatly assisted by the use of project management tools that create Gantt charts (see Chapter 10). Most projects have to be completed by a certain date, so it is helpful to start at the end with the completion date for the project and work backwards, slotting in each task with its dependencies and each of the milestones in turn.

Including the project management tasks in the schedule

Barbara Allan reminds us that

> In addition to the specific tasks that need to be carried out to complete the project you also need to consider the recurrent tasks, i.e. those that are repeated at regular intervals throughout the project. Examples of recurrent tasks might be regular project team meetings, sending out a weekly project news bulletin and updating the project spreadsheet. These recurrent tasks are sometimes

> omitted at the project scheduling stage and they can mean that there is a serious underestimate of the amount of time spent on the project.[2]

Project management and quality management tasks like these should be explicit in the work plan, with clearly identified resources and costs associated with them as well as time allocated to them in the schedule.

Criteria for reviewing the project plan

Here are some useful criteria for reviewing and ensuring the effectiveness of the project plan:[3]

- Does the project plan show the appropriate balance between being comprehensive and complete, and being sufficiently concise to be understandable?
- Is the project plan concise enough to be of practical use for the members of the project board or management team?
- Are all relevant parts of the original project brief reflected in the project plan?
- Is the level of detail in the project plan appropriate for the project, bearing in mind:
  - the duration of the project;
  - the levels of certainty or otherwise concerning the project's final outcomes or products;
  - the complexity of the project, for example the number of departments, partners or separate groups involved;
  - the organisational and business risks involved?
- Is the project plan consistent with corporate and/or programme plans?

The business case

When managing a project it is all too easy to concentrate on *what* is being done and *how* it is being done, while ignoring *why* it needs to be done. The business case states *why* the work needs to be done, and anticipates any problems or threats to which the project could be subject, so that appropriate actions can be taken to deal with them.

The business case is a description of the reasons for the project and the justification for undertaking the project, based on the estimated costs of the project, the risks and the expected business benefits and savings.

Business case development is now an accepted part of project preparation and planning in the higher education sector, and increasingly common when seeking non-operational or external funding in the cultural heritage sector. The PRINCE2 key philosophy is that its business case must drive the project:

> If a satisfactory business case does not exist, a project should not be started. If a business case is valid at the start of a project, but this justification disappears once the project is under way, the project should be stopped. The focus of the business case should be on the totality of business change, not just one element of it – for example, the cost of buying new equipment should take into account the impact on personnel, training, changed procedures, accommodation changes, operational costs, relationships with the public, etc.[4]

Senior management buy-in

The PRINCE2 manual also makes one very important point to bear in mind: the organisational executive or senior management is the 'owner' of the project's business case, not the project manager. It is the executive's responsibility to ensure that the project's objectives, costs, benefits etc. are correctly aligned with the organisational strategy or programme objectives.

This project planning and review period, which must encompass a review of the business case as well as the project plan, is therefore the moment for the project manager to ensure that the appropriate senior management are fully aware and convinced of the business case for the project, that it has received the necessary buy-in at appropriate levels, and that corporate management sees where and how the project will fit into the organisation's overall strategies.

Checklist for reviewing the business case[5]

- Check whether the programme, corporate or strategic objectives that the project is expected to address are still likely to be achievable.
- Check whether recent external or internal events have affected any of the benefits quoted in the business case.
- Establish whether any additional business benefits have become apparent.
- Requantify the benefits where appropriate, and identify any disbenefits.
- Calculate or refine the cost elements, based on the reviewed/revised project plan and the latest information regarding the likely operational and maintenance costs associated with the project.

Monitoring the project plan

I began this chapter saying that planning and re-planning are part of project management that have to be done at regular intervals, and that the project work plan is an essential management tool. Monitoring is the way in which project managers gather information to enable them to measure progress against the project plan.

Monitoring is commonly coupled with evaluation, but the two are very different activities, and I find it more useful to think of monitoring in terms of planning, reviewing and adjusting plans. Project monitoring is an integral part of day-to-day project management. It provides information by which the project manager can identify and solve implementation problems, and assess progress.

The following basic issues need to be regularly monitored:

- Which activities are underway and what progress has been made?
- At what rate are resources being used and costs incurred in relation to progress in implementation?
- Are the desired outputs and outcomes being achieved?
- What changes in the project environment are occurring? Do the project assumptions hold true?

In particular, the monitoring of activities compares the time planned for and actually required to carry out an individual activity. Thus, it can be judged whether the work plan can be adhered to or whether adjustments need to be made. Both milestones and deadlines provide the basis on which the implementation of the project plan is monitored and managed. Whenever individual activities deviate from the schedule, the consequences for other activities and resources must be considered. The causes of these deviations need to be analysed and the timing adjusted. If deadlines for activities that are on the 'critical path' or that influence the timing of other activities cannot be respected, the project manager is required to react by adjusting plans, shifting resources, etc.

Project inputs and outputs need to be available at the time required, in appropriate quantities and of appropriate quality. The time required for making them available is often underestimated. Project management has to ensure that the planning of project activities reflects the time required to mobilise the resources required. Chapters 5 and 6 consider these issues in more detail.

Table 2.1 **Basic steps in monitoring**

Step	Content
1 Collecting data (facts, observation and measurement) and documenting them	■ Indicators for work package, task and activity objectives ■ Quality and appropriateness of activities and use of resources ■ The project environment ■ Cooperation with target groups and partners
2 Analysing and drawing conclusions (interpretation)	■ Comparison of planned and actual achievements (planned and unforeseen) and identification of deviations (review): conclusions ■ Changes in project environment and consequences for the project ■ Comparison of planned and actual mechanisms and procedures of project organisation and cooperation/communication with target groups and partners: identification of deviations and conclusions
3 Making recommendations (judgements) and taking corrective action	■ Adjustment of timing of activities and resources ■ Adjustment of objectives ■ Adjustment of procedures and cooperation/communication methods

Monitoring assumptions and risks

While activities, inputs and outputs are very often regularly monitored, adequate monitoring of assumptions and risks is rather more rarely done. The project manager needs to react promptly if project assumptions do not hold true and jeopardise the success of the project. Chapter 4 deals in more detail with the monitoring and management of risk.

Notes

1. European Commission (2002) *EuropeAid Co-operation Office General Affairs Evaluation. Project Cycle Management Handbook. Version 2.0 March 2002.* Prepared by PARTICIP GmbH.
2. Barbara Allan. *Project Management: Tools and Techniques for Today's ILS Professional.* London: Facet, 2004.
3. Adapted from *Managing Successful Projects with PRINCE2.* London: TSO, 2005.
4. *Managing Successful Projects with PRINCE2.* London: TSO, 2005.
5. Adapted from *Managing Successful Projects with PRINCE2.* London: TSO, 2005.

3

Working in project partnerships

Introduction

In public service and academic institutions, partnerships underpin almost any kind of project. For most externally funded projects and programmes collaboration between a range of different partner organisations is a prerequisite, intended to stimulate cross-sectoral (and in the case of European Commission funding, cross-border) cooperation and maximise the impact and effectiveness of project outcomes. This chapter considers the benefits and challenges of partnerships from a project management perspective, the building and reviewing of working partnerships and project governance structures.

Local government and other partnership policies

> Partnerships are needed because, in most cases, they are the only way most city projects and services can be delivered. A city is made up of organisations, companies and people. It contains pressure groups, special interest bodies and opinion formers as well as excluded groups – all stakeholders in the jargon. It will be subject, especially in a boom, to development pressures at the

> same time as needing to maintain and enhance green space. It must meet statutory requirements as well as promote areas of activity where involvement is discretionary. It may have an informal responsibility for a wider area than its defined physical boundary. All the time, it has to look forward to create a new future, and to ensure that all are involved in decision-making and debate. Finally, it needs to consider the most important stakeholders of all – those too young to participate and those not yet born.[1]

In local government, councils have been working with each other and other local partners for over a century, but over the last three decades, as the Audit Commission observes, 'government policy has moved from encouraging joint working, to effectively making it compulsory.'[2] Local Strategic Partnerships (LSPs) (and other statutory local agreements) are the result, and, while each has a different history, all are voluntary, unincorporated associations that are required to recognise their strategic, executive, and operational roles and organise themselves appropriately. LSPs do not control local public service resources; they have to influence partners' mainstream spending and activity, and they are supposed to engender a culture of partnership working within local authority organisations.

Most projects managed within local authority library, archive or museum services will be framed and influenced by the nature and effectiveness of the LSPs. In many cases there will exist a Partnership Framework document providing guidelines on entering into partnerships at strategic or operational levels – an example from Kent is shown below. Project partnerships should be assessed against such frameworks, no matter how small or large in relative terms the size and cost of the endeavour.

Example: excerpts from Thanet Council's Partnership Framework[3]

Working together for a better Thanet
Version 1 – June 2008

1. Introduction

Partnership working is playing an increasingly important role in effective modern local government activity. To do this, we need to make sure that we are doing the right things, in the right way, at the right time for the right people in an open, honest and accountable manner.

The benefits of partnership working have been the focus for many public, private, voluntary and community organisations recently and the Council has in the past, played a lead role in establishing and developing partnerships. A range of issues have been identified that we need address to ensure that the Council has a consistent and rigorous approach to partnership working, so that we can get the full benefits from it. Clear processes and procedures are necessary to enable us to deliver services to our residents efficiently, effectively and properly with our partners.

The new system of Comprehensive Area Assessment (CAA) being introduced by the government has identified the importance of partnership working, and places stronger emphasis on working with our partners, which we will be tested against. It will focus on the effectiveness of the Council's approach to political, managerial and community leadership, our focus on the people who use our services and whether everyone can access them, our achievements in our shared priorities, and delivering results for our residents through partnership working.

2. Defining a partnership

A partnership is a joint working arrangement where the partners

- are otherwise independent bodies
- agree to co-operate to achieve common goals or outcomes
- create a new organisational structure or process to achieve this goal
- plan and implement a jointly agreed programme, often with joint staff or resources
- share relevant information, and pool risks and rewards

3. Partnership framework

Thanet District Council has an agreed Partnership Framework which deals with the following questions:

- Why do we need to work in this partnership?
- What will the partnership deliver that we could not deliver on our own?
- Is it clear what our role is in the partnership?
- Do we know what the life expectancy is of the partnership?
- Are the aims and objectives of the partnership clear?
- What are the links between the partnership's aims and objectives and the Council's aims and objectives?

Before entering into any partnership, we will assess the potential benefit of the Council's possible participation. We will do this by comparing the objectives and intended outcomes of the proposed arrangement with the Council's own corporate priorities (set out in our Corporate Plan), the priorities of the East Kent Local Strategic Partnership (EK LSP) and the Kent Area Agreement (KA2).

In higher education there are institutional incentives, under a number of government funding programmes, to enter into project partnerships between universities, further education colleges and schools to widen and increase participation in higher education (Aimhigher Area Partnerships, for instance); and to increase higher education's relevance to and engagement with business and employers. The JISC of the Higher Education

Funding Councils provides grants and project funding to stimulate and promote innovation and sharing in ICT solutions in partnerships between higher education institutions that might in other areas be in competition (such as in course development or student recruitment).

And, of course, in collecting organisations such as libraries, museums and archives, strategic and project partnerships between public and private organisations of widely differing kinds are increasingly common to improve knowledge of and access to collections, and to learning and research resources.

Benefits of working in partnership

So if everyone is doing partnership working, what are the perceived benefits of partnership working in projects in our sector? Barbara Allan sees evidence of the following benefits in libraries and information services:

- Enhanced access to people, resources and organisations.
- Enhanced ownership – projects that are set up to collaboratively tackle specific problems are owned by the partners and this means that the project outcomes are more likely to be accepted and owned by the partner organisations.
- Enhanced quality – the involvement of a wide range of people who bring their different professional perspectives can enhance the quality of the project experience and outcomes. Individual partners may be more willing to take on new ideas and working practices as a result of the partnership.
- Increased exposure to new ideas/approaches – working in multi-professional teams can help partners to broaden their outlook and obtain a broader understanding of their work and their context.

- Improved use of resources – partnership working not only enhances access to resources but also leads to more efficient use of resources.
- Enhanced motivation – being part of a successful partnership can boost morale and help individuals to develop new enthusiasm for their work.[4]

With the possible exception of the first, these are all benefits that can be delivered only if the project partnership has been built and managed to maximum effectiveness. Each one of these benefits could just as easily be, or become, negative outcomes: for instance, a project with external partners, funding and timescale that does not integrate into organisational processes can often be *disowned* and sidelined by parent organisations; the involvement of a wide range of people who bring their different professional perspectives to the project, but for whom there are no clearly specified and agreed roles or procedures for arriving at consensus, can result in project outcomes being a political fudge; partnership working, far from making efficient use of resources, is notorious for taking up inordinate and unplanned staff time.

We all work in partnership all the time, with our colleagues and with different departments within our own organisations, where the advantage is that it can (usually) be assumed that everyone shares a particular organisational culture, ethos and goals, as well as the same management and procedures. Our role and place in these everyday collaborations is determined by many things, not least our own personalities and interpersonal skills, our qualifications and experience, and the management structure and style of our workplace.

This possible spectrum of roles is summarised in the University of Wolverhampton's diagram (Figure 3.1).[5] Most would agree that the most unsatisfactory place to be is decidedly at the 'coercion' end!

Figure 3.1 Participation roles

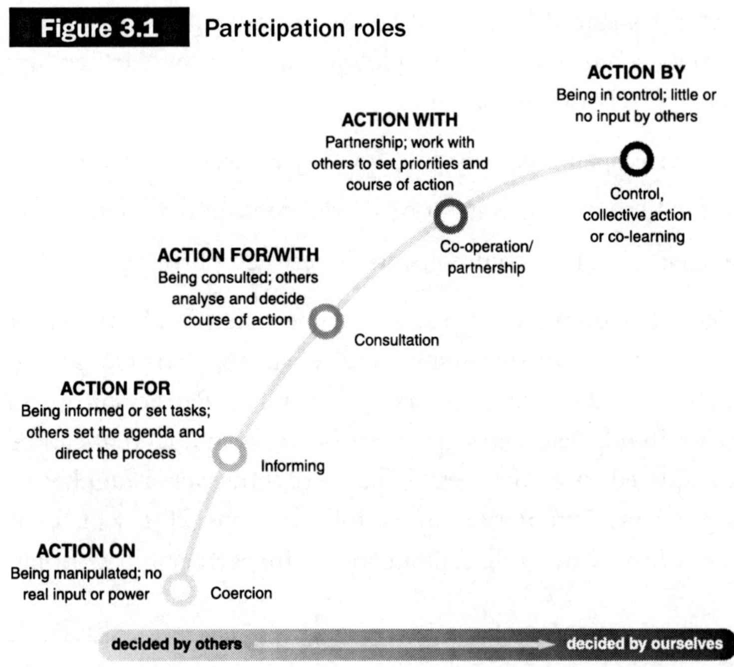

The same factors of personalities, skills, experience and management style are what determine the success or otherwise of partnerships. If any partners – or their representatives within project partnership structures – feel 'manipulated' or coerced, or that they are being consulted while their expectation was that they would be fully included in decision-making processes, the partnership (and therefore the project) is in jeopardy.

Building partnerships

The initial stages of a partnership are probably the most crucial ones in terms of creating a strong foundation for effective working. The more partners and the more complex the project, the greater the amount of time and attention to detail that need to be paid to the initial stages. The project manager has a key role to play in building the partnership, particularly in working to

- create openness, trust and honesty between partners;
- facilitate the agreement of shared goals and values;
- ensure regular communication between partners.

There has been a lot of research undertaken to identify what makes a good partnership and what the barriers are to achieving effective partnership working. Partnerships can work in different ways and there is no one model that can be considered to be the 'best'. There are, however, a number of ingredients, summarised in the following checklist, which – if they are present – will facilitate successful partnership working.

Checklist for building partnerships

- The partnership is agreed and understood by all the partners.
- Shared ownership of the partnership is evident and all the partners feel there is 'something in it for them'.
- There is clear recognition and understanding of the different organisational cultures within the partnership, and these have been accommodated in the partnership structure and project plans.
- A supportive atmosphere already exists within the partnership where suggestions, ideas and conflicts are addressed.

Establishing clear roles

- Are the roles and responsibilities of all partners clearly defined, understood and agreed?

- Is there a lead partner? Is their role clearly defined and agreed?
- Are dedicated time and resources for the administration and operation of the partnership included in the project plan?

Establishing an appropriate structure

- Has the partnership agreed an appropriate constitution and structure? Does it include:
  - *Who employs staff?*
  - *Who administers the day to day activities?*
  - *Who contracts with delivery bodies?*
  - *Which body makes the final decisions?*
  - *Who is responsible for financial control and auditing?*
- Is the membership of committees, working groups etc. defined?
- Are the meetings for the first six months scheduled?
- Are there clear written procedures to prevent conflicts of interest?

Action planning

- Does the partnership have an action or business plan?
- Have those whose job it is to implement the project been involved in negotiating the action or business plan?
- Has the partnership agreed what outputs are to be monitored?
- Has the partnership carried out a risk assessment?
- Is there a clear communications strategy in place?

The choice of partners is vitally important. Partnerships are often formed from existing networks or where there is a history of collaborative work between potential partners. However, there will be circumstances where it will be important to invite new partners to the table: each project demands a partnership with a specific mix of skills, resources and other attributes, and it may be necessary for the project planners (including the designated project manager) to go 'cold calling' on organisations with which they have had little or no contact in the past.

Partnership roles and tasks

Perhaps the greatest area of difficulty in partnership working, particularly when there is no history of partnership between organisations and/or key people in the organisations, is deciding upon the different roles and responsibilities of the partners *and* making sure there are clear boundaries between partners' responsibilities.

Partnership Roles and Tasks[6] is an exercise enabling open discussion and agreement between partners on the partnership structure and responsibilities, including the analysis of how specific project work should be shared between partners, assigning tasks and allocating roles. During the project lifespan there may be changes both to the partners and their roles and tasks; this exercise can also be used to review the partnership at any time and make changes to the structure.

The example in Table 3.1 is based on a project to develop a regional library portal offering seamless access to members of the public to catalogue information from book and archival collections in public libraries, higher education and further education libraries and special libraries in the region. A matrix such as this example is drawn up with the prospective partners listed in the top horizontal row. All the main project activities and tasks are then listed in the vertical left-hand column: I recommend dividing these into those concerned with *the content of the project* (i.e. the intended outcomes – in this example it is a cross-institutional web-based portal),

Table 3.1 **Partnership roles and tasks**

	Lead partner: County Library Service	Partner 1: Regional Library Organisation	Partner 2: Metropolitan Borough Library Service	Partner 3: Academic Library A	Partner 4: Academic Library B	Partner 5: Further Education College Library E
PROJECT CONTENT						
Detailed review of member library requirements	X	O				
User needs research	O		X	O	O	O
Technical development of interoperability tools			X	O		
Design and development of public web interface	X		O			
Pilot and beta-test web-based portal	O		X	O	O	O
Promotion of portal to members and scaling up	O	X				
Public awareness-raising and marketing of portal		X	O		O	O
Evaluation and impact assessment	X		O	O	O	O
PROJECT DELIVERY						
Project governance and strategic planning	X	O	O	O	O	O

(*Continued*)

Table 3.1 **Partnership roles and tasks (*cont'd*)**

	Lead partner: County Library Service	Partner 1: Regional Library Organisation	Partner 2: Metropolitan Borough Library Service	Partner 3: Academic Library A	Partner 4: Academic Library B	Partner 5: Further Education College Library E
Project management		X				
Financial management and control	X	O				
Project monitoring	O	X	O	O	O	O

and those concerned with *the effective and efficient delivery of the project* (e.g. project management). In the former category, the main tasks should be derived directly from the project work plan.

In this exercise it is useful to distinguish between a lead role – i.e. decision-making – and a support role – i.e. being instructed to do the work. This can be done by marking the lead roles with an X and support roles with an O. Once the matrix has been completed, the vertical column under each partner's name can be used as the basis for drawing up a partnership contract or letter of agreement specifying the roles, tasks and responsibilities for each partner. The results of the exercise can also be used to develop and plan the structure of organisations and teams.

The example matrix raises a number of important questions and issues:

- Should the Project Manager always be the same as (or part of) the Lead Partner? In my view, not necessarily. If the Project Manager and the Lead Partner are one and the same (or the Project Manager is embedded within the Lead Partner) there is a risk that the Lead Partner will dominate the project, though this risk will be mitigated by a strong governance structure. On the other hand, a project manager recruited externally, without the insider knowledge and understanding of how to get things done within the lead organisational structure may also present a risk to the project.

- The roles and responsibilities of project partners need to be firmly based upon a dispassionate assessment of the internal competencies, specialisms and capacity of partner organisations. For instance, in this example, Partner 2 has been given responsibility for 'technical development of interoperability tools' because their technical services team has built up considerable expertise and experience in building cross-institutional catalogue access, and has close contacts with key suppliers. More especially, this expertise does not reside in only one member of staff. On the other hand the Lead Partner has worked effectively with the County Council's in-house web design team in a recent redevelopment of the Library Service web-pages, and the team has capacity to take on new design and development work, or has the key contacts to subcontract trusted suppliers.

Governance and management structures

Most projects involve working closely with partners, whether internal or external or a mix of both. Good governance is increasingly recognised as of primary importance to the successful management of partnership working. Governance relates to the way partnerships structure their working relations and can be understood as a set of seven major characteristics with strategies and instruments to ensure their existence: Table 3.2 summarises these:

Table 3.2 **Characteristics of good project governance**[6]

Characteristics	Essential strategies and instruments
Equity and inclusiveness	Statement of the purpose of the project partnership that may also include a broader statement of partners' particular interests.
Responsiveness participation	Stakeholder mapping and analysis: to identify the potential beneficiaries, partners and other stakeholders, and clarify how the partnership will work together to deliver a successful project.
Consensus oriented	Partnership roles and tasks: to clarify the responsibilities and actions of partners and inform the Terms of Reference for each partners' involvement.
Effectiveness and efficiency	A set of relevant reference documents relating to the legal and legislative requirements for the project partnership
Transparency	Standard procedures for recording the proceedings of the project partnership: covering decisions made, communication methods, regular reviews and planning.
Rule of law	Terms of Reference for project partners
Accountability	Quality assurance checks: to maintain and build quality in project objectives, as well as in project management.

Governance challenges

Governance and management structures for project partnerships are often judged, both by those involved and those outside, against the criteria of legitimacy, strategy, and performance.

- Legitimacy: 'Is it fair?' Do the governance arrangements assure confidence that the partnership is a credible and capable vehicle for steering and implementing this project?
- Strategy: 'Is it smart?' Does the governance system enable the partners to set and steer towards agreed strategic goals and objectives?

- Performance: 'Is it effective?' Does the governance system hold the partnership accountable to specific outcomes and criteria for quality, effectiveness, and efficiency?

The most common problems in project partnerships arise in trying to balance these three governance requirements. For instance, overly complex governance systems designed for inclusivity can make it difficult for the project partners to make decisions quickly, and can generate paralysing conflicts and competition among stakeholders.

On the other hand, a single-minded focus on strategic goals, objectives and timelines can deliver impressive results, but without clear provision for inclusive participation the project partnership might be at risk of capture by the most powerful actors.

In a challenge to accountability, project partnerships that have put in place strong project management and executive teams may perform efficiently but partner representatives on the governance board become remote from the action and concerns about equity and accountability become secondary to the efficient delivery of targets.

Project partnership governance structures

The Audit Commission in the UK observes that

> a one-size-fits-all approach to governance is inappropriate for partnership working. Governance arrangements must be proportionate to the risks involved. Public bodies need to strike the right balance between protecting the public pound and ensuring value for money. At the same time, they need to manage the risks of innovation without

> inhibiting the innovative potential that emerges when organisations collaborate.[8]

Most project partnerships with external partners are unincorporated associations. The Audit Commission stresses the importance of the partnership's governing document and suggests that partners might adapt the Charity Commission's model constitution. The main elements of this are:

- the name of the partnership;
- aims and objectives;
- membership, including status of different members and termination of membership;
- schemes of delegation;
- powers;
- roles;
- income;
- meetings: notice and frequency of meetings; quorum rules; chairing arrangements; voting arrangements; and representation of other members;
- decision-making processes (scope and timescales);
- timescales;
- amendments to the partnership's rules;
- minutes; and
- exit strategy/arrangements for dissolution.

Partnership management challenges

> The many organisations in the public domain are the shared expression of collective purpose. In principle,

> therefore, they are in a co-operative relationship. The reality can be different. Organisations have their own dynamic and those who work in them have their own purposes. Health and local authorities seeking their separate purposes can easily deny collective purposes. Different parts of the same organisation may be in competition for public funds.
>
> Management involves the management of interaction between different agencies and organisations. Management has to examine how, while recognising the reality of competition, the practice of co-operation can be enhanced.[9]

Project partnership management shares many of the challenges encountered in operational and service management. Even if good governance structures have been established, project partnerships are subject to external and often conflicting influences and deeply dependent upon the personalities, skills and experience of the people designated to represent the interests of individual partners within the established structure.

The project manager is rarely in overall charge of governance structures: the chair of the project board is most likely to be a senior manager from the lead organisation, or an external appointee. Indeed, the project manager may have had no role in building the partnership in the first place and no say at all in who is nominated by each individual partner to represent their interests and manage their inputs. However, an effective project manager should be influential in identifying and addressing (or orchestrating appropriate responses from others) critical partnership management challenges. If these are ignored they will inevitably have a detrimental effect on the successful implementation of the project.

Here are some typical partnership management challenges identified by Barbara Allan.[10]

- *Dominance in the partnership of one member or organisation:* all too often this can be dominance by the lead organisation in the project. Such dominance can lead to resentment by other partners and it runs completely counter to the essential inclusiveness of a good project partnership.
- *Rotating project board members and other partner representatives:* it is a problem if one or more partners are represented at project meetings by different members of staff throughout the life of the project. As in any team-building exercise, the project partnership team needs to cohere around individual personalities, strengths and experience: changing team members prevents this essential coherence from emerging.
- *Unequal distribution of work or project responsibilities:* this is a fundamental issue that needs to be addressed in the early stages of identifying partner roles and responsibilities. Clarity and consistency is essential. If a small number of people take on the majority of the work in a project they may end up feeling resentful that they are carrying other partners. It can also result in other partners losing 'ownership' of the project. An experienced project manager can soon spot any imbalances in workload or responsibilities and draw them to the attention of the chair of the project board before inequalities become entrenched.
- *Added bureaucracy:* working in partnership undoubtedly can add another level of bureaucracy to the project work. At the very least, partnership working involves meetings and careful documentation of events, which can often take up more time and resources than necessary. These are

inescapable facts and need to be faced and accepted as part of the partnership process, though efforts to minimise unnecessary procedures and work lie at the heart of good project management.

- *Political interference:* partnership working is highly political, driven as it is by government and institutional policies, and often incentivised by project funding opportunities. Very often the partnership itself attracts high expectations and political attention (as opposed to the project purpose), placing it under an uncomfortable spotlight. The project partner organisations will all have wider strategic goals and purposes that may also exert pressures on a project partnership over time, and lead to the 'interference' in the project by senior managers or other stakeholders.

Working across different cultures and sectors

Barbara Allan notes that working in project partnerships frequently, and perhaps increasingly, involves people from a range of cultures working together – from different organisational cultures, different countries and different generations. There are significant implications for effective project management in this cross-cultural working. Even within local authorities internal partner departments can have very different working cultures, as the example below from Bristol illustrates.

> Responsibility for BCDP [Bristol Cultural Development Partnership] in Bristol City Council up to 2000 was with the arts unit in Leisure Services, even though cultural planning covers more than the arts (the original proposal to be placed in the chief executive's unit was never implemented). A good relationship was developed

> with Planning, Transport and Development, though this was informal; a more formal relationship was attempted with Education, but this failed – a disappointment given the role of education in developing culture but perhaps not surprising given the crisis Bristol's education service finds itself in. Relationships have improved greatly now that the departments of leisure and planning have merged, though there is more to do. Only when partner organisations recruit staff experienced in working in partnership, or put their staff through partnership training programmes, will this be resolved.[11]

The following checklist of barriers to co-ordination between potential partner organisations (for projects, local and regional development, and service delivery) will be familiar to many in library, museum and archival services.

Barriers to co-ordination[12]

Structural

- fragmentation of service responsibilities across agency boundaries, both within and between sectors;
- inter-organisational complexity;
- non-coterminosity of boundaries;
- competition-based systems of governance.

Procedural

- differences in planning horizons and cycles;
- differences in accountability arrangements;
- differences in information systems and protocols regarding access and confidentiality.

Financial

- differences in budgetary cycles and accounting procedures;
- differences in funding mechanisms and bases;
- differences in the stocks and flows of financial resources.

Professional/cultural

- differences in ideologies and values;
- professional self-interest and autonomy;
- inter-professional domain divergence of views;
- threats to job security;
- conflicting views about user interests and roles.

Status and legitimacy

- organisational self-interest and autonomy;
- inter-organisational divergence of views;
- differences in legitimacy between elected and appointed agencies.

Notes

1. Andrew Kelly and Melanie Kelly. *Managing Partnerships*. Bristol Cultural Development Partnership, 2002.
2. National Audit Commission. *Working Better Together? Managing Local Strategic Partnerships*, Crosscutting National Report. April 2009. Online at: *http://www.audit-commission.gov.uk/lsp*.
3. Thanet District Council Partnership Framework. Online at: *http://www.thanet.gov.uk/council_democracy/governance/partnership_working/3_partnership_framework.aspx*.
4. Barbara Allan. *Project Management: Tools and Techniques for Today's ILS Professional*. London: Facet, 2004.
5. Adapted from *Introduction to the Programme and Project Cycle: Training Handbook*, CIDT, 2002, University of Wolverhampton.

6. Adapted from Freer Spreckley. *Project Cycle Management Toolkit*, ed. Sally Hunt, 3rd edn. Local Livelihoods Ltd., 2006.
7. Adapted from S. Rochlin, S. Zadek and M. Forstater (2008) *Governing Collaboration: Making Partnerships Accountable for Delivering Development*. London: AccountAbility.
8. Audit Commission. *Governing Partnerships: Bridging the Accountability Gap*, Public Sector National Report, 2005.
9. David McKevitt and Allan Lawton. *Public Sector Management: Theory. Critique and Practice*. London: Sage, 1994.
10. Allan, op. cit.
11. Kelly and Kelly, op. cit.
12. Adapted from 'What is successful partnership and how can it be measured?' in C. Glendinning, M. Powell and K. Rummery (eds) *Partnerships, New Labour and the Governance of Welfare* (2002), quoted in *Beyond Boundaries: Citizen-Centred Local Services for Wales. Review of Local Service Delivery: Report to the Welsh Assembly Government*. 2006.

4

Risk management

Introduction

All projects are about changing something and all change incurs risk.

> Risks are about the project not going to plan. They are about resources and people not being available when you want them, about machines not working, about the outputs not being of the quality you were expecting. This can happen because of an unchecked assumption, or a lack of realism in the planning, or poor organization or because you are trying to do something which is new and/or complex. If you are dependent on resources or factors outside your control the project is risky.[1]

On the other hand, some amount of risk-taking is inevitable if the project is to achieve its objectives. Risk can be viewed as the reverse of opportunity: if there is uncertainty of outcome it could lead equally to a positive opportunity as to a negative threat. Something may simply turn out differently to how it was expected or planned. This view allows the possibility that risks can be turned into opportunities if managed effectively. The task of the project manager is to manage the project's exposure to risk, the probability of specific risks occurring and the potential impact if they did occur.

What does risk management involve?

Arguably, risk management is the single most important component of project management. PRINCE2 considers that it involves having:

- access to reliable, up-to-date information about risks;
- decision-making processes supported by a framework of risk analysis and evaluation;
- processes in place to monitor risk;
- the right balance of control in place to deal with those risks: that is, where the possibility of a risk occurring is balanced against the costs of limiting that risk.

In a project with a short timescale (one to two years) there is less likelihood that a risk can be turned into an opportunity: for example, if a project partner decides about halfway through a project to leave the project consortium, it may be regarded by other partners as a positive decision, allowing them the opportunity to bring in new approaches or competences. However, the project timescale may not allow much time for doing this effectively and the project is likely to be exposed to considerable new risks if such a significant change is pursued.

Elements of risk management

JISC infoNet provides a particularly appropriate approach to risk management for academic and cultural heritage organisations in their toolkit:[2] this breaks down risk management into a number of iterative sub-processes:

- risk identification
- qualitative risk analysis
- quantitative risk assessment
- risk response planning
- risk monitoring and control.

Figure 4.1 JISC infoNet's view of risk management

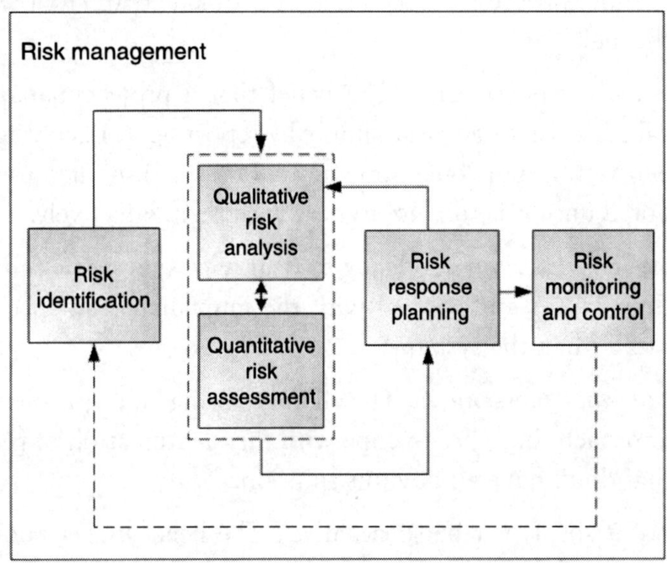

Management and institutional attitudes to risk

The project manager, though responsible for managing risk within the project, also relies on the active support of institutional managers (and those not only from their own institution or the lead project partner). Management attitudes to risk can cause problems or, indeed, constitute a risk to the project. JISC infoNet offers the following examples:

Extreme risk aversion: Procrastination in decision-making. This often means that some possible options/opportunities are no longer feasible.

Pass the buck: Inability to reach closure on difficult decisions. Issues discussed regularly by a range of committees without progress. Decisions not documented and followed through.

No news is good news: The belief that a project manager causes a risk or an issue simply by reporting it. Encourages people to report only good news. Often risks/issues aren't noted until it is too late to deal with them effectively.

Knee-jerk reaction: Tendency to deal with symptoms rather than causes and to deal with the immediate and specific rather than the systemic.

Shoot the messenger: The 'Don't bring me problems' approach. Inability to cope with the identification of risks that don't have an obvious solution.

Make it so: 'Don't be so negative'. The belief that a poorly conceived or inadequately resourced project can be made to succeed by sheer force of will.

Initial risk identification and analysis

Risk analysis must take place when the business case for the project is established and during the initial project planning stage. At that stage the project manager (assuming she or he was involved) will have considered the question, 'What could go wrong, how likely is it to happen and how severe would the effects be?'

A good project manager will assume that the implementation of the project will *not* go absolutely according to plan, and therefore make reasoned judgements about how exposed the whole initiative might be if changes occur and how likely those changes might be.

Typical questions for the planning stage are:

- If it takes 5 per cent extra time to implement a particular activity will deadlines still be met?
- If there is a price increase in equipment procurement might budgets be exceeded?
- If the project fails to keep to its planned time schedule could it mean resources required at some later stage of implementation would not be available?
- Does the effectiveness of particular activities rely upon the actions of other people and are they capable of carrying out what is required? Are there any personal or political reasons why they may not behave as expected and required?
- What external factors could throw the project off course?

Techniques for assessing risk

Risk checklist

Compiling a risk checklist is a useful technique for assessing potential risks to the project and determining whether they are likely to be high, medium or low risks. The checklist usually comprises lists of pairs of opposing statements – one signifying low risk and the other high – with a scale between them. The example in Table 4.1, adapted from Liz MacLachlan's book,[3] shows a list of risk statements with a scale along which the project might be placed and a weighting score depending upon how important a particular risk might be to the project. The multiplication of each of these figures gives an overall risk score.

Table 4.1 **Example of a risk checklist**

Low risk	Scale 1 2 3 4	High risk	Weight 1–6	Total
Full-time experienced project manager	1	Inexperienced or part-time project manager	5	5
Project team experienced and has appropriate skills	2	Team is inexperienced and lacks some skills	3	6
Staff are dedicated to the project	3	Staff have other duties	4	12
Installation of a system which has been used elsewhere	1	Installation of a new system	3	3
Core business will not be affected	4	Project will have a significant impact on core business operations	5	20
Little constraint on completion date	4	Mandatory completion date	4	16
Suppliers are well-established and experienced	2	Suppliers are new or one-man businesses	2	4
No dependence on other projects outside manager's control	3	Heavy dependence on other projects outside manager's control	5	15
Totals	20		31	81

Risk analysis template

For its project plans JISC requires risk analysis based on a template reflecting the key areas of risk, as shown in Table 4.2.[4]

This template requires the project planner to list the potential risks; assign a probability to each risk (1 is low, 5 is high); assess the severity should the risk occur (1 is low, 5 is high); give each risk a score (probability × severity); and for the highest scoring risks, plan how they can be prevented from happening (or manage them if they occur). Table 4.3 provides an example of the analysis of risk associated with undertaking an evaluation of strategic programmes in UNESCO's Communications and Information sector.

Table 4.2 **JISC risk analysis template**

Risk	Probability (1 – 5)	Severity (1 – 5)	Score (P × S)	Action to prevent/ manage the risk
Staffing				
Organisational				
Technical				
External suppliers				
Legal				

Fishbone diagram

Another approach to analysing the cause and effects of potential risks is to use an Ishikawa or fishbone diagram. The effect to be improved or removed is written in a box at the right-hand end of a long arrow. The possible causes of that effect are then listed and connected to the effect like

Table 4.3 **Example of a risk analysis using the JISC template**

Risk	Probability	Severity	Score	Action to prevent/ manage the risk
Active collaboration of UNESCO staff at all levels may not be assured, constraining the evaluation's access to documentation, data and key informants	3	5	15	Seek early assurances from CI sector managers of this collaboration during Inception stage. Specify early the key informants to be approached, and key documentation required.
Data regulations may prevent access by evaluation team to UNESCO e-mail distribution and alerting lists to facilitate survey distribution.	5	3	15	Arrange with UNESCO staff to send out e-mailed survey alerts on behalf of evaluation team.
Tight timetable specified for the evaluation allows for little flexibility in approaching key regional and country informants.	4	3	12	Documents required from country/ regional offices clearly communicated as early as possible. Follow up 'missed' contacts by telephone.

bones connected to the backbone of a fish. It is then possible to look at all of the factors relating to that cause. The level of detail required will vary according to what is being analysed. The more specifically the effect is stated, the easier it will be to pin down the causes.

Figure 4.2 An example of a fishbone diagram

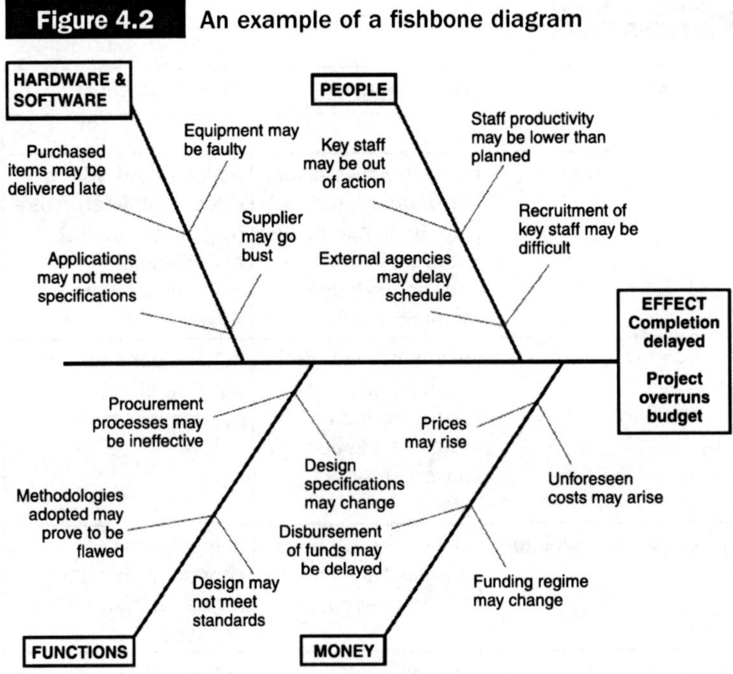

The example in Figure 4.2 has a very broad effect – project delay – and in reality there would be many more bones on the fish.

Risk categories and factors

Risks can be categorised in a number of ways that usually reflect internal and environmental risks. For instance, risks and their effects are categorised by DFID's Tools for Development handbook[5] into external, financial, activity and human resources – see Table 4.4.

Table 4.4 Identified categories of risk

Categories	Risk at source	Risk as an effect
External		
1. Infrastructure	Infrastructure failure prevents normal functioning (e.g., key staff unable to attend work due to transport strike).	Actions have adverse effect on infrastructure (e.g., overload communications systems such as email).
2. Economic	Economic issues such as interest rates, exchange rates or inflation adversely affect plans.	Actions generate an adverse effect on economic issues.
3. Legal and regulatory	Laws or regulations may limit scope to act as desired.	Inappropriate constraint through regulation may be imposed.
4. Environment	Environmental constraints limit possible action.	Actions have a damaging effect on the environment.
5. Political	Political change requires change of objectives.	Actions give rise to need for a political response.
6. Market	Market developments adversely affect plans.	Actions have a material effect on the relevant markets.
7. 'Act of God'	Ability to act as desired affected by (e.g.) flood, earthquake	Contingency plans against disaster scenario prove inadequate.
Financial		
8. Budgetary	Lack of resources to carry out desirable actions.	Inability to control or direct resources.
9. Fraud or theft	Resources not available to carry out desirable actions.	Resources lost.

10. Insurable	Insurance not obtainable at acceptable cost.	Failure to insure against insurable risk leads to loss.
11. Capital investment	Poor investment limits scope for future action.	Inappropriate investment decisions made.
12. Liability	The organisation is damaged by others' actions leading to the organisation gaining a right to seek damages.	A third party acquires a right to damages against the organisation.
Activity		
13. Policy	Policies are founded on flawed background information.	Inappropriate or damaging polices are pursued.
14. Operational	Unachievable/ impractical objectives.	Objectives not achieved or inadequately achieved.
15. Information	Inadequate information leads to decisions being made without sufficient knowledge.	Information available for decision making lacks integrity and is not reliable.
16. Reputational	Reputation may limit scope to act as desired.	Development of poor reputation.
17. Transferable	Risks which could be transferred are retained or are transferred at wrong price.	The cost of transferring risk outweighs the risk transferred.
18. Technological	Technology failure (e.g. IT system) prohibits operation as planned.	Need to improve/ replace technology to maintain effectiveness.

(Continued)

Table 4.4 **Identified categories of risk (*cont'd*)**

Categories	Risk at source	Risk as an effect
19. Project	Projects are embarked upon without the associated risk being properly assessed.	Projects fail to deliver either within assigned resource or in functionality or outcome.
20. Innovation	Opportunity to use new approaches embarked upon without appropriate identification of associated risk.	Opportunities for gain from innovation missed.
Human Resources		
21. Personnel	Lack of suitable personnel with appropriate skills limits ability to act as desired.	Personnel adversely affected in terms of morale or loyalty.
22. Health and safety	People unable to perform their responsibilities due to health issues.	Damage to the physical or psychological well-being of people.

In the library, museum and archive world – dominated by public or academic sector organisations – categories of risk factors might typically also include the following.

- *Knowledge-base*: It is important to understand the knowledge level of partners on all aspects of the project. In technology based projects this might be, for instance, in the area of metadata, digitisation, or legal issues. Failure to develop common levels of understanding may lead to a lack of involvement by some partners, buy-in on later aspects of the project, or in the long run to a delayed or failed project.

- *Project complexity*: It is quite common for projects in our sector to become overly complex, often because of inexperience on the part of project planners or project managers. Complexity can arise when, for instance, a project has too many objectives to be achieved within a limited timescale or budget; or there are too many activities scheduled for the same time period and requiring inputs from the same stakeholders; or there is an insufficiently specific and rigorous project plan, which leaves open the possibility of changes and 'mission drift' during implementation. Technical complexity can be particularly risky, especially when only one partner is responsible for the technology support to the project, and other partners become frustrated with delays or confused by options and issues.[6]
- *Organisational environment*: Risks may relate to the organisational culture; for instance, a project based on innovative change will be inherently risky in a bureaucratic or conservative institution. Specific risks are also associated with current institutional circumstances: some examples of circumstances that may cause risk to a project include:
  - a similar project has failed in the past;
  - the organisation is being restructured whilst the project is in progress;
  - many related projects are going on without effective programme management;
  - there is about to be a new postholder in one or more senior management positions;
  - one or more core IT systems are changing;
  - expansion/merger/location moves are taking place.
- *Technical barriers*: It is unlikely that all project partner organisations and designated project staff bring either the same levels of technical knowledge or experience of compatible systems. Relatively simple and predictable

things, such as staff needing technical support to use a range of equipment and software in the project, or the use of different firewalls by the collaborating partners, can cause technical problems and therefore pose risks.

Legal issues

Early consideration by the project manager of the potential legal issues that may arise during the project is advised, and it is a good idea to do so in collaboration with the relevant experts within partner organisations, such as human resources staff. Four legal areas in particular are associated with risk:

- *Employment:* the level of risk may depend upon whether the project will draw its staff from existing employees of partner organisations (on secondment, part-time release from normal duties etc.) or whether short-term contract staff will be recruited (by the project board as a legal entity, by the lead partner organisation or individual partners). A range of UK and European legislation may need to be taken into account.
- *Health and safety:* legislation may need to be taken into account if project staff are recruited by a legal entity set up for the purposes of the project, and not by lead or individual partners in the consortium.
- *Data protection:* in particular, risks may arise associated with data protection if the project plan includes any market research or user needs assessment work, which may involve using surveys, or gathering personal data (both facts and opinions) from the public.
- *Copyright and intellectual property issues:* many projects draw upon content or material written and produced by

third parties, particularly in the development of printed and electronic publications or websites. Risks arise in the use and management of this material where, for instance, written permission for use from the copyright holder has not been obtained.

Risk tolerance and risk thresholds

Before determining what to do about risks, the project partners and the project manager must consider the amount of risk they are collectively prepared to tolerate. This will vary according to the perceived importance of particular risks. For example, the view of financial risks and how much the project team is prepared to put at risk will depend on a number of variables, such as overall organisational budgets and the potential effect on other parts of a programme or organisation. The project board may be prepared to take comparatively large risks in some areas and none at all in others, such as risks to health and safety.

Risk tolerance can also be related to other tolerance parameters – for example, risk to completion within timescale balanced against the need to achieve quality in project outputs.

The risk tolerance of an organisation will lie somewhere on the spectrum shown in Figure 4.3 from risk averse to actively risk seeking.

Figure 4.3 **JISC infoNet's risk tolerance spectrum**

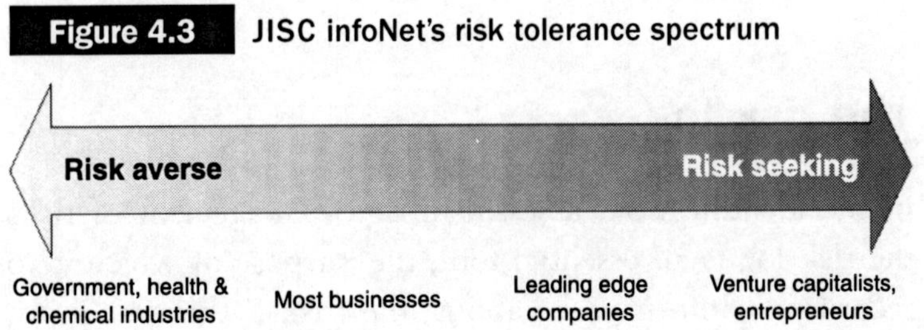

Most academic and cultural heritage institutions lie towards the risk averse end of the spectrum and view risk as something to be avoided at all costs.

> The risk averse mind set often results in the expectation from senior management that a Project Manager's role is to remove risk. This is not the case. Managing risk is not the same as removing it and risk management is undoubtedly easier in the right type of supporting culture.[7]

Consideration of levels of risk tolerance within a project partnership should also lead the project manager to establish the specific levels of acceptable and unacceptable risk for this particular project, giving them a yardstick by which to measure risks as they arise and make judgements about possible responses. These are called 'thresholds' for qualitative definitions about risk and, once determined, they can be quantified in a risk assessment template (see the example in Table 4.2 above). What, for instance, is meant in a particular project by medium risk? If a risk is likely to cause a five-week delay to the project or cost £10,000, where does that sit on the scale of 'very low' to 'very high'? These threshold definitions are essential to determine high cost and time implications for the project before risks can be assessed in a meaningful way. Table 4.5 provides an example from the academic sector.

The risk log

In the identification, assessment and management of risks the risk log is an essential tool, the purpose of which is to record all information about the risks, their analysis,

Table 4.5 **General measure of impact**[8]

Impact	Cost	Time	Quality
Very low	Variations manageable by moving funds between project budget lines	Slight slippage against internal targets	Slight reduction in quality/scope with no overall impact on usability/standards
Low	Requires some additional funding from partner(s)	Slight slippage against key milestones or published targets	Failure to include certain 'nice to have' elements or 'bells and whistles' promised to stakeholders
Medium	Requires significant additional funding from partner(s)	Delay affects key stakeholders and causes loss of confidence in the project	Significant reductions in scope or functionality will be unavoidable
High	Requires significant reallocation of partner(s) funds or borrowing to meet project objectives	Failure to meet key deadlines in relation to the strategic plan	Failure to meet the needs of a large proportion of stakeholders
Very high	Increases threaten viability of project	Delay jeopardises viability of project	Project outcomes effectively unusable

mitigation measures and status. Whether the risk log is a document or spreadsheet (perhaps part of a database), it should include the following elements:

- risk identifier (unique)
- author (who identified the risk)
- date identified
- description

- risk category (for example, knowledge base, organisational, technical)
- impact
- probability
- proximity
- countermeasure(s)
- owner
- date of last update
- current status (for example, reducing, increasing).

Obviously, when the risk log is first opened much of this information may not yet be available. The effective use of risk logs depends upon regular review and updating of information; they are a fundamental part of a systematic risk management framework. This point is illustrated by the JISC infoNet example of a risk log template from the academic sector in Table 4.6, which includes a cost element dependent upon decisions being made and recorded about the response to the risk.

The risk profile

A risk profile is a way of increasing the visibility of risks and assisting management decisions about suitable responses. It is normally given a graphical representation showing two axes of **probability** and **impact** and uses weighting scales for low to high probability and low to high impact. The example in Figure 4.4 doubles the numeric value each time on the impact scale, giving more weight to risks with a high impact. A risk with a low probability but a high impact is thus viewed as much more severe than a risk with a high probability and a low impact.

Table 4.6 **A risk log template**

Unique ID	This may be simply a title but some kind of alphanumeric coding is likely to be useful where you are dealing with a large number of risks.
Description	**Condition** – 'There is a risk that' **Cause** – 'Caused by' **Consequence** – 'Resulting in'
Probability	What is the likelihood of the risk occurring? It would be helpful to record the justification behind this analysis.
Impact	What will the impact be if the risk occurs? It would be helpful to record the justification behind this analysis.
Timescale	What is the 'risk window' when this risk may occur and when do you start to lose options as to how you respond?
Cost	What will the risk cost if it does occur? NB You can't assess this unless you know what your response action will be.
Owner	There should be a person nominated to 'own' the risk which means monitoring the situation and ensuring that necessary management actions are carried out. In a project situation this should be somebody within the project team and in all cases it should be somebody who will be impacted by the risk and who has a vested interest in addressing it.
Management approach	What are the agreed response actions? These may be broken into: ■ preventative actions to mitigate the risk and ■ the response action if the risk actually occurs. This is sometimes known as an 'Impact Plan'.
Residual risk	This is the expected level of risk once all the mitigating actions are complete.
Early warning signs	What 'trigger' might alert you to the fact that the risk is about to occur? In some cases you may only choose to spend money on a response action once the trigger occurs.

Figure 4.4 A risk profile

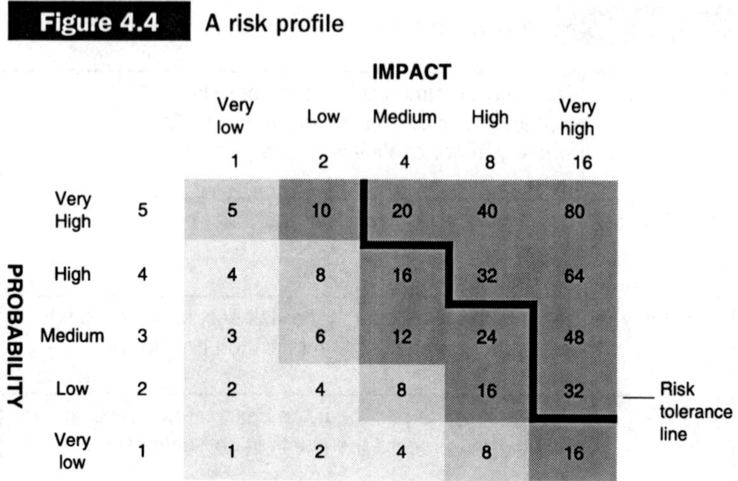

The project manager and project board will decide where the risk tolerance line for the project should lie, above which risks would be referred upwards by the project manager.

Suitable responses to risk

Having identified the risks, both below and above the risk tolerance line, the project manager needs to take a view on what the response to each risk should be. The range of responses is fairly standard across different project management frameworks and methodologies. Table 4.7 provides a summary.

Risk response actions may be preventative measures taken as soon as a risk is identified, and not only when a risk actually occurs. The project manager will ensure that actions are recorded in the risk log and the status of the risk is re-assessed once the preventative or mitigating actions are complete.

Table 4.7 **Summary of typical risk responses**

Response	Description
Avoidance or prevention	Terminate the risk by doing things differently and thus removing the risk, where it is feasible to do so. For instance, there is a plan to build a new library and archival storage facility on a greenfield site but there is a risk that the council will refuse planning permission and delay the project. The project partners decide to build on brownfield site on a former industrial estate. This incurs additional cost in terms of demolishing old buildings and removing hazardous waste.
Mitigation or reduction	Take action to control the risk in some way where the actions either reduce the likelihood of the risk developing or limit the impact. For instance, the project will not easily be able to attract the required technical staff, so a salary supplement is offered to project staff.
Transference	Moving the impact (and ownership) of the risk to a third party, via for instance an insurance policy or outsourcing services. For instance, the project board is aware that colleges are the target of an organised gang stealing hardware. A decision is taken to outsource some of the project servers to a hosting company.
Acceptance	Tolerate the risk, perhaps because nothing can be done at a reasonable cost to mitigate it or the likelihood and impact of the risk are at an acceptable level.
Contingency	Dealing with the risk via contingency rather than altering the plan. Actions are planned and organised to come into force as and when a risk occurs.

Risk responsibilities

While the project manager is normally responsible for ensuring the risks are identified, recorded and regularly monitored and reviewed, the project board should also have responsibilities. PRINCE2 defines these as:

- notifying the project manager of any external risk exposure to the project;

- making decisions on the project manager's recommended reactions to risk;
- striking a balance between the level of risk and the potential benefits that the project might achieve;
- notifying corporate or programme management of any risks that affect the project's ability to meet corporate or programme objectives.[9]

Notes

1. Liz MacLachlan. *Making Project Management Work for You*, The Successful LIS Professional Series, ed. Sheila Pantry. London: Library Association Publishing, 1996.
2. JISC infoNet Risk Management Toolkit. Online at: *http://www.jiscinfonet.ac.uk/InfoKits/risk-management/printableversion.pdf*.
3. MacLachlan, op. cit.
4. JISC Project Management Guidelines 2008. JISC Executive. Online at: *http://www.jisc.ac.uk*.
5. DFID. *Tools for Development: A Handbook for Those Engaged in Development Activity*, Version 15.1. 2003. Online at: *http://www.dfid.gov.uk/Documents/publications/toolsfordevelopment.pdf*.
6. N. Allen and L. Bishoff (2002) 'Collaborative digitization: libraries and museums working together', *Advances in Librarianship*, 26: 43–81.
7. JISC infoNet, op. cit.
8. Adapted from JISC infoNet Risk Management Toolkit, op. cit.
9. *Management Successful Projects with PRINCE2*. London: TSO, 2005.

5

Managing human resources within a project

Introduction

Human resource management for project managers has some specific characteristics that differentiate it, in emphasis and scope at least, from operational human resource management. Project managers will typically work within a framework of governance structures that lie outside their own organisational structures, and which are very likely to include people from external partner organisations.

The project inputs and behaviour of all the people contributing to the project, including those of project boards and steering groups, must be 'managed' to meet specific project timetables and targets. The project manager will be responsible for managing multi-stakeholder partnerships as much as managing the project team itself.

This chapter highlights some of the particular challenges in the multi-partner project context, addresses the competences required for effective project management and project team building, and considers organisational culture and how it can affect the way people work.

Orchestrating decisions

The project manager is very likely to find him or herself in a situation where they need to 'orchestrate' major decisions to be taken by the project board or steering group. Glass[1] advises that, rather than just trying to explain to the key people the logic of the decision-making case, a more thought-through approach, which takes account of the political and cultural realities or your project partnership and governance structures, is more likely to be effective. He suggests a five-step process (see Figure 5.1).

Identifying the 'decision network' depends upon classifying the key people within the project organisations and the main roles they play in the governance or delivery of the project. These people may or may not be on the project board or steering group; for example, a key figure may be a senior manager within one of the partner organisations, who does not sit on the project board itself but controls a particularly vital department or function within a partner organisation. This may be quite a challenge if the project has a number of external partners represented on the board or steering group, all with important and influential decision-makers.

In a decision network, key people can be categorised as, for example:

- authoriser – not directly involved in making the decision but with the power to sign off or veto it;

Figure 5.1 Orchestrating a major decision in a five-step process

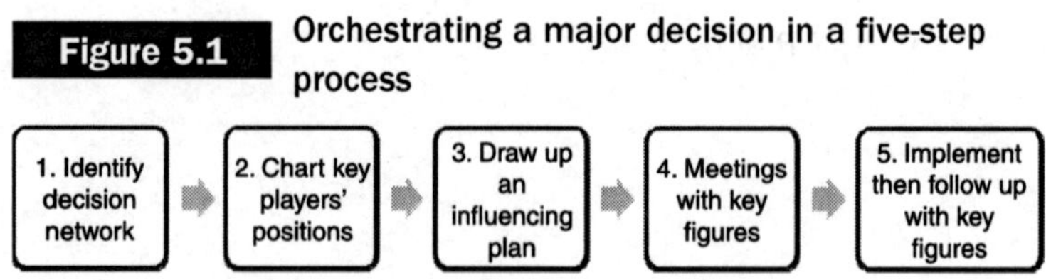

- owner – will take the decision or be responsible for presenting it to the project steering group;
- gatekeeper – can control access to key figures, resources or messages;
- key influencers – people to whom the owner might look for support or who have influence over the authoriser;
- influencers – as above, but with less say in the matter than do key influencers.

Charting these key players' positions means assessing their current view of the issue requiring a decision, identifying what might motivate them to change that position if necessary and how best they might be influenced or approached to do so. The influencing plan will flow from this assessment and determine the project manager's actions to orchestrate the favourable decision. Glass emphasises the importance of face-to-face meetings with each of the key figures, for which the project manager must have the appropriate communication skills and personal self-confidence to be effective.

Keeping in touch with the key figures, once the favourable decision has been made and the project is back on track, is the positive final step, to check if they are satisfied with the results or project progress, and to 'leave the door open' in case there is a next time.

Knowledge, skills and attitudes required by project managers

A good project manager needs wider-ranging knowledge, human resource management and other skills than might normally be expected of middle managers within a library, museum or archive organisation. Table 5.1 summarises this

Table 5.1 Desirable knowledge, skills and attitudes of a project manager[2]

Knowledge and understanding	**Skills and experience**
Personal Own strengths and weaknesses Sources of help and support	Personal Assertiveness Management of stress Management of uncertainty Time management Presentational skills
General management Own organisation and parent body (e.g. local government), including roles and responsibilities of key people Politics, power and culture of project organisations Change management Legal aspects of human resource management Legal issues e.g. health and safety, copyright	**General management** Strategic management Human resource management Financial management Management and motivation of teams Ability to communicate with and influence senior managers General communications skills Marketing and promotion
Project management Project management frameworks (e.g. PRINCE2) Overview of project management process Sources of funding Sources of information and support on general project management issues	**Project management** Project management tools and techniques Bids and proposal writing Business plan creation Budget management Research skills, e.g. design of an evaluation process Risk analysis
Professional Policy context for library, museum and archive service delivery Professional context, e.g. own library and information or museum service, services in other sectors Professional networks	**Professional** Technical expertise e.g. library and information management, museums and archives management, curatorial skills, collection management, digitisation Subject expertise Knowledge management
Other The context and working practices of organisations in other sectors (e.g. government organisations, private sector)	**Other** Working with different professions, organisations, and sectors **Information and communication technology (ICT)** Use of project management software Use of full suite of office software Use of Web 2.0 tools
Attitudes Flexible; Diplomatic; Positive; Persistent; Reliable; Hardworking; Enthusiastic; Unflappable; Good attention to detail.	

wide range of attributes desirable in a project manager. Perhaps the most fundamental are:

- Knowledge and understanding of their own organisation and parent body (where appropriate), especially if this is the lead organisation of the project partnership: There are risks involved in recruiting a project manager from outside; lacking this insider knowledge and a network of contacts, they may struggle to be effective, at least initially.
- Knowledge, understanding and working experience of organisations in other sectors – especially essential if the project is owned by a multi-stakeholder partnership, with external partners from different sectors contributing staff to project governance and the project team.

Contextual issues in managing the project's human resources

There are two broad contextual issues that the project manager needs to consider and understand to manage the people in a project:

- cultural differences between partner organisations, that might have a significant impact on the success of a project team;
- change management principles, since almost all projects delivered in public sector organisations are catalysts for delivering profound changes and many are associated with the introduction of technologies that change the way people work in very fundamental ways.

Organisational cultures

. . . say you have two project managers:

- Project manager A is technically brilliant and can solve problems which would make even the best of his colleagues tremble in their rubber-soled suede shoes, but is not very good at handling organisational politics or at motivating staff.
- Project manager B is technically OK but certainly not as good as A, but she can play the organisational structure like a Stradivarius, making it do exactly what she wants. Getting the best resources, the right facilities, executives' agreement is second nature to project manager B.

Which one would you give your key project to?[3]

Organisational culture can be deep and pervading and every organisation, even within the same sector and same line of business (e.g. university library services), feels different. The differences are palpable in the physical surroundings (buildings, office arrangements, decoration, etc.), the way people behave (polite, helpful or condescending, busy, stressed or at ease, interested, bureaucratic, etc.), and the way they think (proactively problem-solving, pedantically sticking to the rules, hierarchical, overcome in any given situation by a kind of hopeless victim mentality). Everyone has encountered organisations where they feel immediately at home and others where the mismatch between them and the organisational culture is palpable.

Roger Harrison's[4] four main types of organisational culture are as true today as they were when written, and can serve as a useful starting point for thinking about how an organisation's power and political processes work, although no organisation is likely to fall clearly into just one of these categories and within organisations there are often departmental sub-cultures.

- Power (autocracy) – a single person or small group leads the organisation, which may be entrepreneurial or a not-for-profit, with little in the way of formal structures. As it grows in size it often has trouble in adapting and can start to fall apart. Characterised by a high level of political activity as the leaders become surrounded by 'courtiers' eager to attract attention.

- Role (bureaucracy) – in this organisation it is not who a person is but what position s/he holds that is important. Things are done by the rules; loyalty is appreciated; individualism and dynamism are discouraged. Role cultures appear to offer security and stability but they are unable easily to adapt to change in their environment. Political success comes from knowing how to play the system.
- Task ('adhocracy') – an organisation built around temporary teams, in which people form a team, carry out a task and then disband to form different teams for the next task. It relies to a large extent on people 'playing fair' and can easily break down into infighting over key resources or high-profile tasks.
- Person (democracy) – this organisation (often associated with law firms or academic institutions) to an extent allows each individual to follow their own interests, while maintaining mutually beneficial links to the others.

> Power is the basis upon which most organizations function. Those who understand the uses of power will tend to prosper, while those who disregard them will be continually surprised as their proposals are sidelined in favour of suggestions coming from people who succeed in acquiring some form of power.[5]

Working with different national cultures

Barbara Allan[6] makes the point that project work in the cultural heritage sector can also often involve working together with people from a range of different national as well as organisational cultures. Culture in this sense includes unconscious values, for example ways of behaving with other people, different working and social practices that project managers need to take into account if they are working across national boundaries. These might have an impact upon:

- the extent to which people think of themselves as individuals or members of a group;
- the distance between managers and workers and the importance of hierarchy; in many countries workers tend to be afraid of their managers and leaders (who tend to be paternalistic and autocratic);
- gender relations; for example, attitudes towards working with and being managed by male or female staff;
- the extent to which people prefer unstructured and unpredictable environments as opposed to structured and predictable ones;
- time orientation and attitudes towards time pressures and deadlines.

Change management

All projects are about change of some sort, and are often part of a programme dedicated to quite profound organisational change and its management. The larger the scale of a project, the more change management issues must be explicitly addressed in project planning and implementation. In particular technology-driven projects without sufficient change management processes included in the plan run the risk of functioning well at a technical level, but being underused or failing to achieve their true value.

Change management is too large a subject to be addressed in detail in this book. Nonetheless, in terms of human resource management within project structures, the following process checklist[7] highlights the key focus areas for a project manager engaged in a change management programme or initiative.

The eight-stage process of creating organisational change

1. Establish a sense of urgency. Examine market and competition realities. Identify and discuss crises, potential crises, or major opportunities . . . change won't occur where there is complacency.
2. Create the guiding coalition. Pull together a group with enough power to lead the change, and urge them to work together as a team. No one person has the credibility, expertise or skills to provide the necessary leadership alone.
3. Develop a vision and strategy. Provide a vision that gives the change effort direction and motivates people.
4. Communicate the change vision. Use every vehicle possible to get the message out: big or small meetings, memos and company newsletters, formal and informal interactions. Communicate the vision in terms that will be understood in a five-minute discussion.
5. Empower broad-based action. Change those systems or structures that seriously undermine the vision. Emphatically encourage risk taking and non-traditional ideas, activities and actions.
6. Generate short-term wins. Plans for visible performance improvements and early evidence that sacrifices are worth it. Recognise and reward people who make wins possible.
7. Consolidate gains and produce more change. Use increased credibility to change all systems, structures and policies that don't fit together and don't fit the transformation vision. Reinvigorate the process with new projects, themes, and change agents.
8. Anchor new approaches in the corporate culture.

The project team

> A team is a small number of people with complementary skills who are committed to a common purpose, performance goals, and approach for which they hold themselves mutually accountable.[8]

Projects by their very nature demand a team approach to staffing and benefit greatly from successful recruitment and effective management of the team sustained throughout the life of the project. The project team are the people who are actually going to do the work of delivering the project outcomes, or oversee its delivery by staff from partner organisations or external suppliers. Building a coherent team and a sense of ownership and shared responsibility within the team is even more vital, and possibly more challenging, in a multi-partner project because team members are very likely to be located within different partner organisations.

Typically in cultural heritage sector projects the project manager is unlikely to be able to recruit many of the project team members externally or even to select the team members themselves from within partner organisations. It is much more likely that one or two (perhaps technical) staff may be externally recruited but the other team members will be nominated by their organisations or departments or be the obvious and only qualified choice for a particular role within the team.

However the team is brought together, it will be the project manager's job to motivate them individually and make the team cohere as an effective working unit. The fundamental differences between typical operational work and project work in libraries, museums and archives should be borne in mind: Table 5.2 summarises different characteristics of the work from the point of view of a project team member.

Table 5.2 **Differences between operational and project work**

Operational work	Project work
is predictable	is unpredictable
is repetitive	is unique
is standardised	may be difficult to standardise
takes place in predictable time period	takes place in estimated time period
maintains the status quo	results in change

Independent, cooperative and collaborative ways of team working

There are necessarily different types of project team and their nature is dependent on much more than the particular management style of the project manager or lead organisation. For instance:

- The project team may be physically split up between different organisational or geographical locations, only coming together for project team meetings, and some of these may be 'virtual' meetings.
- Most project team members are unlikely to be dedicated full-time staff, but they will be undertaking project work in addition to their day jobs. Project team members therefore will still be mainly 'owned' and paid by their operational functions or departments. There is always the risk that functional managers prioritise functional activities over project work, with the result that projects suffer.
- The nature of the project work itself could dictate the way the team might work together; for example, there may be quite large 'sub-teams' focused on specific work packages that relate only at very particular points to other project work.

Barbara Allan recommends that it is worth thinking carefully about how best to organise the work and the project team to suit the particular requirements of your project. She suggests that a project team might work independently, cooperatively or collaboratively, each of which demands a different management approach (see Table 5.3).

Table 5.3 Different types of working in a project team[9]

	Independent	**Co-operative**	**Collaborative**
Definition	Individuals work by themselves on their own tasks. They each have their own goal.	A task is divided into sections and individuals are responsible for their own piece of work. They each have their own goal.	The team works together on the task. They are working towards a shared goal.
Types of tasks	Organising room bookings. Acting as a contact person.	Writing a project report.	Producing a project plan. Writing a project report.
Effective management	Individuals are briefed and deadlines are agreed. Individuals report back to PM and/or team meetings.	The whole team is briefed and deadlines are agreed. Division of work is agreed. Boundaries between tasks are clarified. Individuals agree how they will communicate with each other and deal with critical or unexpected circumstances.	The whole team is briefed and deadlines are agreed. Individuals discuss and agree how they will work with each other. Future meeting dates are set for collaborative work to take place.

Team building

Most people reading this book will be familiar with at least one of the many team-building models. Tuckman's[10] model of how groups form is probably the best known.

Orientation (forming)

The initial formation of the group. People will tend to be polite and careful. Members will be torn between being cautious about expressing any strong views and being anxious to make an impression. They will be testing the water and will probably not make any real progress with the group's main tasks.

The project manager can facilitate team members through this stage by:

- establishing an open environment for teamwork;
- facilitating learning about one another;
- providing clarification to the team on their project purpose and deliverables;
- encouraging participation by all team members;
- providing structure to the team by assisting in task and role clarification;
- establishing norms for interaction;
- encouraging open communication among team members.

Conflict (storming)

The group starts to work. As their comfort level rises, members put their views forward much more forcefully. The initial consensus breaks down. There can be disagreements about the tasks, arrangements made in initial meetings, operating methods, leadership – everything can quickly be called into question. Conflicts stemming from personality or functional approach break out. If this stage persists, some members will become frustrated at the lack of progress and withdraw mentally or physically. If it is controlled, the group can productively redefine its objectives, approach and ways of working.

Project managers can facilitate team members through this stage by:

- assisting team members to establish norms that support effective communication;
- encouraging team members to share their ideas about issues;
- facilitating conflict reduction.

Collaborating (norming)

As members start to resolve style and character differences, they begin to find ways of working together. A new unofficial hierarchy can arise, a set of unwritten codes of behaviour gradually forms, norms for managing tasks and conflict develop.

Project managers can facilitate teams through this stage by:

- talking openly about issues and team members' concerns;
- encouraging team members to give feedback.

Productivity (performing)

The project team is now a cohesive unit: individual members know and accept their roles, they associate with the group's interests rather than their own personal agendas, people start to bond and they can now usefully make progress with the tasks they were formed to address.

These phases are recognisable in all project teams, but reaching the 'norming' and 'performing' stages for a project team can be particularly challenged by:

- teams made up of people from different organisations;
- typical short term timelines for project completion;
- team members with a 'day job' who are only part-time dedicated to the project;
- all too common turnover of key project staff;
- external dynamics of the parent organisations.

Internal and external dynamics

Much of the analysis of team performance has concentrated on the teams' internal dynamics – how members work together, how conflict is handled, what roles people adopt and so on. But many of the problems which can hamper team performance come as much from the relations between the project team and the project partner organisations as from within the team itself.

Projects and project teams often start in a flurry of activity. But as daily operational problems occupy people's attention, it becomes increasingly difficult for the team to get access to the required skills or resources – key people are busy, managers have other things on their mind and so on.

One way of trying to avoid these situations in a project is to begin with a 'goal redefinition' exercise to clarify what is expected of the project and the project team and the implications for each partner organisation. This could be done through the project manager undertaking one-to-one interviews with senior managers who are not involved directly in the project in each partner organisation, but who are nonetheless 'key influencers', finding out their expectations and what would and would not be acceptable. These interviews should include questions such as:

- What are your expectations from the project and the project team?
- What would you like to see change as a result of the project team's work for your area?
- What are the main dangers/traps facing the team? How could we avoid these?

Interface management

The project manager also needs to establish a clear and formal structure around

- how the project team interfaces with the rest of the organisation within which it may be embedded (e.g. the lead organisation in the project partnership);
- its own project management structures (already developed as part of the project initiation); and
- other key stakeholders in the project, such as community or user groups, other local government departments (see Figure 5.2).

Successful project teams, like any other task-oriented teams, rely to some extent on creating their own community: the members need to transfer at least a degree of loyalty to the project and their team and develop ways of working which can be specific to the team. In doing this there is a high risk that the project team can become isolated from the rest of the lead organisation within which it may be embedded and the other project partner organisations for which it works.

Figure 5.2 **Interface management: support structures around project teams**

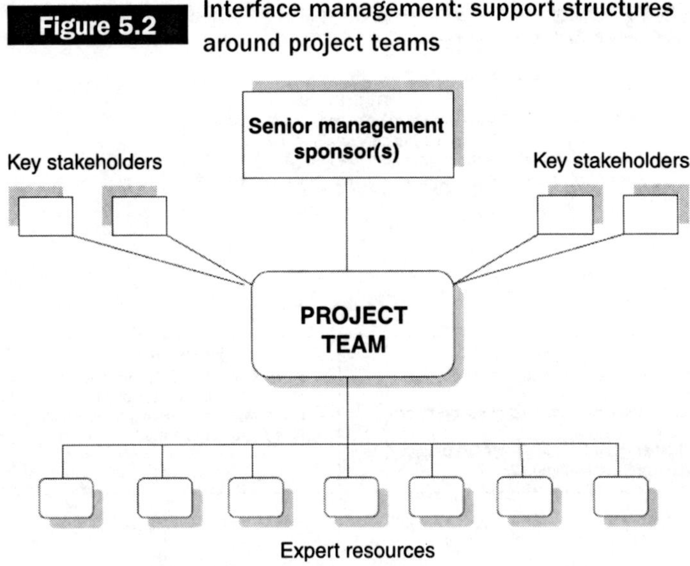

Operational staff and managers in these organisations may begin to view project team members as separate or exclusive, pursuing goals and using methods that are not those of the organisation itself.

If the project team slips out of sync with its parent organisation or partners, the emotions and hostility that can be generated may put concrete progress in the project in jeopardy. This is where the project manager's 'influencing plan', as discussed earlier in this chapter, can come into its own. It is the role of the project manager to communicate regularly with the key organisational people to keep them informed of project progress and test the water for the organisation's responses. The project manager must be the first to recognise that the project team, or sub-teams within different partner organisations, is being judged in a negative light.

Glass suggests there are three dimensions along which an organisation will judge any team – rational, political, emotional (see Figure 5.3). Unless all of these three aspects

Figure 5.3 Interface management: how project teams can be judged[11]

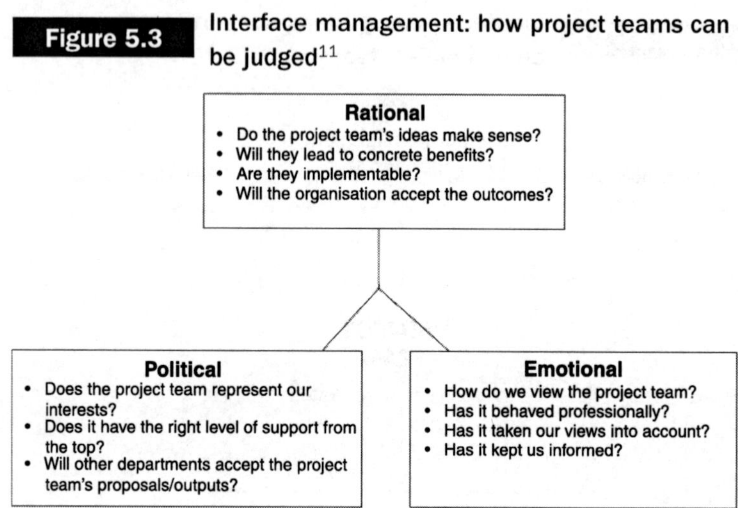

are carefully balanced and managed the team risks ending up with its proposals being rejected by the very organisation it thought it was helping.

Team communication

The ways in which communication flows within the project team can be critical to its success and productivity. The project manager should seek to achieve balanced, open communication between all members, although this is often difficult to achieve due to personality and organisational issues (for instance, members with similar interests or from one function are likely to stick together).

For example, if everything seems to pass through the project manager (in relatively small projects likely to be the only team leader) this probably slows down decision-making and limits the exchange of ideas. On the other hand, in projects with several partner organisations and, potentially, sub-teams, it is easy for cliques to form, within which the project team members communicate intensively among themselves but infrequently with the rest of the wider project team.

Team motivation

Because of the typically short timescales of projects, and the fact that project team members are likely to come from a number of different project partner organisations (or, if the project is an internal project, from several different departments and grades), the project manager usually lacks recourse to the standard checks, balances and levers of people management – performance appraisal, coaching and mentoring, job and business process reviews, etc. This makes the task of understanding the personality types in the project team and motivating project staff (or reinforcing their own motivation) to achieve project goals even more important.

Guidelines on team motivation include the following key approaches to staff motivation:

- Keep a positive attitude, even if things are not going well.
- Show confidence in the project team members.
- Listen to, support and help all team members.
- Ensure good informal contact (daily) within the team, using technology to overcome location and time barriers.
- Ensure good planning so that everyone knows what to do, how and when to do it, and is working to the same schedule.
- Make sure that promises given about plans, schedules and costs are kept.
- Minimise bureaucracy.
- Deal with team problems and complaints quickly, within the team, even if this is difficult or painful.

Table 5.4 **Key factors in ensuring success in project team management**[12]

Negotiating success criteria	Understanding what it will take to deliver the project outcomes and integrating this with the abilities and interests of individual team members.
The team together	Ensuring that the team works productively when together by establishing and agreeing basic codes of conduct and procedure.
The team apart	Ensuring that team members are kept informed when working apart, and retain their commitment to the project.
Membership contributions	Ensuring continued commitment by valuing individual contributions and delegating leadership roles where possible.
Leading the team	Keeping the team moving forward by setting realistic targets and achieving motivation.
Continuous planning and review	Constantly reviewing the project plan in the light of changing circumstances or amended stakeholder expectations, and keeping members informed of any changes.
Managing the outside	Keeping key influencers in project partner organisations 'onside' and keeping suppliers and subcontractors 'in tune' with the project in order to avoid problems arising from poor quality or delays in contributions.

Notes

1. Neil M. Glass. *Management Masterclass: A Practical Guide to the New Realities of Business*. London: Nicholas Brealey, 1998.
2. Adapted from Barbara Allan. *Project Management: Tools and Techniques for Today's ILS Professional*. London: Facet, 2004.
3. Glass, op. cit.
4. Roger Harrison. 'How to describe your organization', *Harvard Business Review*, September–October, 1972.
5. Glass, op. cit.
6. Allan, op. cit.
7. J. Kotter. *Leading Change*. Boston: Harvard Business School Press, 1996 (quoted in *African Schoolnet Toolkit*, published by the Commonwealth of Learning and SchoolNet Africa).

8. J.R. Katezenbach and D.K. Smith. *The Wisdom of Teams: Creating the High Performance Organization.* Boston: Harvard Business School Press, 1993.
9. Adapted from Allan, op. cit.
10. B.W. Tuckman. 'Development sequence in small groups', *Psychological Bulletin*, 63: 1965.
11. Adapted from Glass, op. cit.
12. Adapted from DFID. *Tools for Development: A Handbook for Those Engaged in Development Activity*, Version 15.1. 2003. Online at: *http://www.dfid.gov.uk/Documents/publications/toolsfordevelopment.pdf.*

6

Managing other project resources

Introduction

All project managers know that nothing ever goes exactly according to plan in a project, and a good project plan will include contingency planning based on sensible risk analysis. However, accurate estimating of resource requirements in the project planning stages is also essential if the project manager is to be able to manage project resources effectively during implementation, without having to make radical adjustments to the planned activities 'on the fly'. If, for example, the project planners underestimated the amount of time required to implement tasks, the project manager will have no choice but to cut something, or to spend more money on doing it differently – remember the essential characteristics of a project: time, costs and performance (see Figure 2.1). One of these cannot be changed without affecting one or both of the others.

If the project plan was sufficiently realistic and robust, the management of resources other than project staff in implementation is mainly about effective monitoring, reviewing and revising those plans in response to external events. The resources discussed in this chapter are:

- time
- money
- subcontractors and suppliers.

Because the planning stage is so important to effective resource management within a project, a number of critical factors and useful techniques for planning project resources are revisited here.

Time

Underestimating the time it takes to get things done is perhaps the most common error by inexperienced project planners. The other side of that coin is that, when a project has a timescale for completion imposed on it (for instance, by the funding organisation), it is all too common for planners to try to cover too much within the time and resource limits.

Getting accurate estimates of the time required to do each task in a work plan (duration and effort), and ensuring that the project schedule has enough slack and lag time built into it (elapsed time), are the two key issues. If the project manager has an opportunity to influence these plans, or to revisit them before projects start, these are the two areas to focus on and amend if necessary and possible.

Estimating time

The thing to remember about estimating time is that it depends upon human resource capabilities – an individual's response to getting things done within a certain timeframe. JISC infoNet makes the point that

> the accuracy of those estimates depends quite simply on the extent to which you have done something similar before. Where you are getting into activities that are outside the skills and experience of the project team, the accuracy of the estimates decreases and the level of risk involved increases . . . It is important that all members of the team understand the need for estimation in the project plan. If they fail to do so then they could become demoralised – viewing inaccurate estimation as failure. Where estimates are wrong the team needs to discuss the reasons for this in a positive manner so that all members of the team can contribute to increasing the accuracy of future estimates.[1]

The other point to bear in mind is that accurate estimating of time required allows the project manager to set realistic deadlines for project tasks. Being realistic about deadlines is especially important if the project team is made up of staff from different project partner organisations who are not dedicated full-time to the project.

The JISC infoNet suggests that there are likely to be three possible responses when asking someone how long it will take to do something; see Table 6.1.

To overcome this people should be asked to give three figures: their most optimistic, their most likely and their most pessimistic estimates: this is the PERT method of estimating task duration (see Chapter 2).

Scheduling, precedence diagramming and the critical path

Most project planning software packages use the 'precedence diagramming' method for scheduling project tasks. This method plots the tasks to be completed and connects them

Table 6.1 **Possible responses on how long it will take to do something**

Padding	Where individuals try to give themselves extra time by inflating the estimated duration to ensure they can complete the task 'on time', e.g. they think it will take one week, they say it will take two weeks.
Accurate	Where individuals give an honest appraisal of how long they think the task will take.
Squeezing	Where individuals either want to curry favour or are worried that the truth will be poorly received so they reduce the estimate to a level they are almost certain to fail to complete on time.

with arrows that show the dependencies. Mandatory dependencies are inherent in the work or process: for example when constructing a new website, developing the way the site works is dependent on having appropriate and relevant content. Discretionary dependencies are those defined by the project manager and their team, based on best practice or previous experience. Once the dependencies are agreed they can be mapped into a precedence diagram (see Figure 6.1).

Figure 6.1 **Precedence diagram**

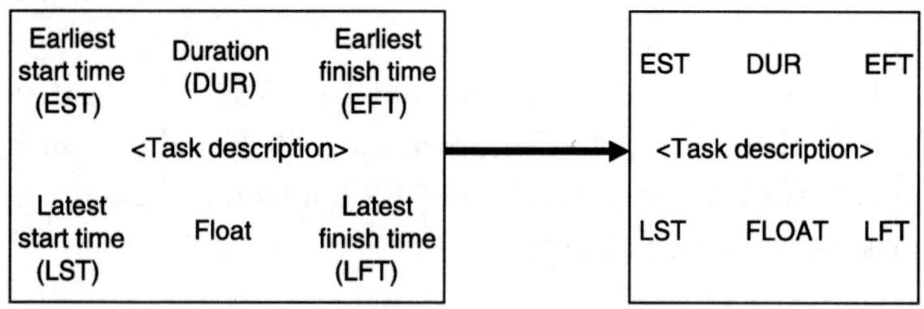

When compiling the diagram a task is normally represented as a box, and tasks are linked with arrows to show any precedent. There are no loops and, at any stage, all preceding tasks must be complete before the following task can begin.

To schedule in detail the following information about each task is required:

- The duration (DUR) of each activity – how long it will take to complete.
- The earliest start time (EST) – the earliest an activity can start without interfering with the completion of any preceding activity.
- The latest start time (LST) – the latest an activity can start without interfering with the start of any subsequent activity.
- The earliest finish time (EFT) – the earliest an activity can finish.
- The latest finish time (LFT) – the latest an activity can finish without interfering with the start of any subsequent activity.
- The 'float' time of an activity – the time available to perform the activity less the time needed i.e. time available minus activity duration.

The critical activities are those with zero float: that is, for a critical activity EST = LST.

A critical path appears on any precedence diagram and links tasks which have no float. A critical path can be traced through the project from start to finish.

Monitoring project progress

In monitoring project progress the project manager is interested in the comparison between what the plan shows should be happening at the time now and the actual state of the project at the time now. The differences between actual and estimated resources are called 'variances'.

When variances in the project are identified and quantified the project manager will need to make a judgement about how they affect the rest of the project. Variances are not always bad news – some tasks may be completed ahead of time, so slack can be introduced elsewhere in the schedule.

If a task on the critical path has slipped in some way then it must be dealt with as a priority. There are two main ways to do this – either increase resources or decrease the amount of work that can be done.

Increasing resources

This can take several forms:

- Subcontract particular tasks.
- Increase the number of people available to work on a task.
- Allow the team to work overtime.
- Increase the overall duration of the project and keep the same number of staff active.

Decreasing work

Decreasing work content of the project can be more problematic because that may require deviating significantly from the original aims and objectives. It means:

- deleting tasks;
- putting two or more tasks together to find a resource gain;
- identifying existing work that may be used as a building block.

Time management

Time management is a common and general human resource management issue. It is particularly critical in a time-limited project. It is certainly a good idea to set up from the start some good project procedures and management tools relating to time management – e.g. keeping bureaucracy to a minimum; everyone using the same methods for recording things; document management; everyone communicating with the same software, etc., and using technology to overcome the need for frequent travel to meetings.

As with any good manager, a project manager should try to make sure that all the project team works cleverly to manage their time, to identify anyone who is challenged and offer training or appropriate advice. The project manager may have limited influence where project team members are staff members in partner institutions or in departments within their own institution where they have no management remit. Building good relationships with the key stakeholders and influencers in partner institutions, being aware of where the (seasonal) pressure points may be in project partner organisations and building flexibility into the project timetable to accommodate these are all ways to mitigate problems arising from pressure on time.

The project manager should be a good time manager her/himself and set an example through prioritising work effectively, knowing how much time it takes to get something done, and running meetings to time. This may entail analysing how they spend their time and implementing a few time-saving methods that will gain them the most time.

The following are examples of time savers with particular relevance in a project context:

- Managing the decision making process, not the decisions.
- Establishing daily, short-term, mid-term, and long-term priorities.
- Ensuring all meetings have a purpose, time limit, and include only essential people.

- Maintaining accurate calendars and abiding by them.
- Knowing when to stop a task, policy, or procedure.
- Delegating everything possible and empowering subordinates.
- Ensuring time is set aside to accomplish high-priority tasks.
- Using checklists and to-do lists.
- Adjusting priorities as a result of new tasks.

Money

In the same way that effective management of time within a project can depend upon how accurate and realistic the project work plan was, management of finances also depends upon accurate and realistic project budgets.

Preparing budgets

Preparing a budget is an integral part of establishing the business case for a project. An evaluation of the financial requirements is central to establishing whether the project is viable or not. In cases where external funding is being applied for, the budget will form an important element of the project proposal.

The budget is likely to change as project activities are implemented. It is therefore useful for the project manager to undertake an early analysis of what likely impact any change in costs and income may have on the overall budget and assess whether the project is high or low risk in financial terms.

The types of costs incurred in a project will be split between capital or one-off costs and operational costs. Table 6.2

Table 6.2 **Main project cost headings within an academic context[2]**

Cost heading	Issues to consider
Hardware	Is it more cost effective to buy or lease? If purchasing will you pay up-front or enter into a financing agreement?
Software	How many licences are required in each phase of the project? Are future annual increases capped?
Equipment	Is it more cost effective to buy or lease? Do you need maintenance agreements, e.g. for printers, etc?
Project staff	Include recruitment costs, e.g. advertising or agency fees. Include employers on-costs, e.g. pension and national insurance. Where staff are on incremental pay scales allow for annual increments. Allow for annual pay increases. Do you need to allow for overtime working? What will happen at the end of the project – do you need to build in redundancy payments?
Other staff time	Do you need to reimburse other departments for staff time assisting the project, e.g. porters moving equipment, IT staff overtime, staff attending meetings or training?
Consultancy	Are consultants paid a daily rate or a fee for the job? What are their daily travel and expenses limits? Where will they be travelling from and how often?
Staff development	What training is required at each stage of the project and for how many people? Can you save money by advance block booking of external training? Is it more cost effective to train on-site rather than pay travel costs? Are there any online training materials available?
Office overheads	Include any chargeable items such as heating, telephones, security, postage, etc.
Travel	Include travel to meetings, conferences and training courses.
Hospitality	Will you be required to provide catering, for meetings or training events?
Consumables	Stationery, printer cartridges, etc.
Contingency	What is a reasonable contingency estimate given the amount of risk and uncertainty in the project?

shows some of the major cost headings and suggests issues to think about when trying to cost those items.

Transparent approach to costing (TRAC) or 'full economic costing'

Project managers in UK higher education or other areas of the public sector will be aware of the government's introduction, since 2000, of the transparent approach to costing or TRAC. TRAC has introduced some new processes and activities in institutions that sit alongside existing accounting and project-management systems. The most notable are the requirements to allocate academic staff time, and to build up the cost of research projects on a 'full economic cost' (fEC) basis. If project partner institutions use TRAC methods then the project budget itself must build on these and comply with TRAC requirements.

Time allocation in TRAC has been the most contentious issue, but it is essential if partner organisations are to plan for academic or other staff contributions to a project and how these costs can be funded. Institutions are also required to use TRAC to allocate non-staff costs (such as space, libraries, etc.) using robust methods, and to develop their own charge-out rates for space and major facilities, and for residual indirect costs. Every UK higher education institution, for instance, is supposed to have a TRAC Project Manager who typically has attended a number of briefing and training sessions and has been involved in benchmarking with peer institutions as an aid to TRAC implementation. They would be potentially useful resource persons for project planners and project managers within academia. TRAC guidance is now all consolidated into a single searchable web-based guide for those involved in implementation of TRAC.[3]

The essential elements of calculating the fEC of a project consist of

1. directly incurred costs: such as the costs of research staff, technical and clerical staff costs and non-staff costs (consumables, equipment purchase, etc.);
2. directly allocated costs: such as partners' senior management and other collaborators' time and costs for contributions to the project, facilities and estates costs, or charges for laboratory technicians and major research facilities;
3. indirect costs (including the cost of capital employed).

The fEC of a project is not dependent upon what an external funder or sponsor will pay, which is the price. The difference between the fEC and the price is the institutional contribution from the lead partner or collaborating project partners, or the institutional surplus available for re-investment.

The JISC provides instructions on handling fEC to organisations bidding for project funding in the UK[4] and a sample budget template (Table 6.3).

Table 6.3 **Adapted JISC example budget for project bids submitted by UK higher education institutions**

Directly incurred staff	**Year 1 total**	**Year 2 total**	**TOTAL £**
Post, grade, no. hours & % FTE	£	£	£
Post, grade, no. hours & % FTE	£	£	£
Post, grade, no. hours & % FTE	£	£	£
Total directly incurred staff (A)	£	£	£

Table 6.3 **Adapted JISC example budget for project bids submitted by UK higher education institutions (*cont'd*)**

Directly incurred non-staff	**Year 1 total**	**Year 2 total**	**TOTAL £**
Travel and expenses	£	£	£
Hardware/software	£	£	£
Dissemination	£	£	£
Evaluation	£	£	£
Other	£	£	£
Total directly incurred non-staff (B)	£	£	£
Directly incurred total (A+B=C) (C)	**£**	**£**	**£**
Directly allocated	**Year 1 total**	**Year 2 total**	**TOTAL £**
Staff	£	£	£
Estates	£	£	£
Other	£	£	£
Directly allocated total (D)	£	£	£
Indirect costs (E)	**£**	**£**	**£**
e.g. interest on capital loans			
Total project cost (C+D+E)	**£**	**£**	**£**
Amount requested from JISC (or other external funder)	**£**	**£**	**£**
Institutional contributions (i.e. from project partners)	**£**	**£**	**£**
Percentage contributions over the life of the project	JISC × %	Partners × %	Total 100%

Reviewing and reporting on budgets

Reviewing and reporting on the budget is a routine part of project management. The project manager is likely to be working within an approved budget and indicative 'tolerance limits' for financial risk. There may also be contingency funds set aside to cover specific anticipated risks.

Table 6.4 **Example of monthly project outgoings**

	April	May	June
People	1700	250	4600
Equipment	50	0	25
Expenses	0	0	15
TOTAL	1,750	250	4,640

Regular monitoring of the project budget entails looking at the project plan and working out what will be spent when, to give a figure against which to monitor what is actually spent – see Table 6.4.

A critical factor to bear in mind is the difference between when invoices are presented for payment and when the money actually goes out of the project budget. To be accurate the second figure is the one to use, so the project manager needs to know how quickly the lead partner pays its bills. This is particularly important at the end of the financial year, where typically in the public sector money not spent may be lost.

Many project managers find that their original budget included as part of the project proposal does not match with the reality of running the project. Estimates of expenditure may differ from the actual expenditure. For example, a project manager may have estimated a cost of £2,100 on software and £5,400 on hardware but then once the project is up and running find that they need to spend £1,000 on software, £3,500 on hardware and £2,000 on specialist furniture (the latter not being included in the original budget).

In this situation the project manager can sometimes approach the funding organisation and ask permission to vire or transfer the funding from one budget heading to another. It is vital that all the paperwork is retained, even if it is only an e-mail approving the change, as it may be required for audit purposes.

Project managers are usually required to report financial information to the project board on an 'exception-reporting' basis, with the focus on things which are significantly at variance with the original budget. When any major discrepancy occurs, the project manager is charged with the responsibility to identify why the variance has happened and whether it constitutes a systemic failure. Appropriate corrective action can be agreed and implemented.

Most financial reporting makes no immediate allowance for project tasks and activities being performed early or late. If things are going well and outputs are being delivered early, then the project may be spending money quicker than planned. Conversely, if the project is behind schedule operationally, costs may not have been incurred by the planned dates, so expenditure figures look artificially good. As long as any variance can be explained it is quite normal to review and update the budget at appropriate intervals in order to reflect actual activity.

Subcontractors and suppliers

'Projects typically need stuff,' as Joseph Phillips puts it, 'servers, software, subject matter experts . . . etc. And to buy all this stuff, you need to go through procurement processes.'[5] Typically, projects in libraries, museums and archive organisations will need to subcontract external consulting and expert services (for instance, to undertake market research, specialist studies, evaluations and reviews), procure technical services (such as digitisation of print or visual materials) and purchase hardware and software.

The procurement processes allow the project manager to identify which project requirements can best be met by purchasing and acquiring products or external services, including

- consideration of whether, how, what, how much, and when to acquire;
- consideration of potential vendors;
- identification of any existing formal and informal procurement-related policies, procedures or guidelines that might be used in the project;
- consideration of the contract types to be used for the supplier of different products and services.

The process also includes the preparation of the procurement documents. The initial and critical document is the specification or statement of work or terms of reference, which describes the thing or service that is required. It is unfortunately quite common for projects in the cultural heritage sector to procure, for instance, consulting services on the basis of poorly thought-out and vaguely specified terms of reference. The results of these exercises can often be unsatisfactory or less than completely useful to the project.

The specification is provided to the potential supplier or suppliers as the basis of an invitation to bid or tender (sometimes also known as a 'request for proposals' or RFP). An RFP requires a price for the work, but also suggestions and ideas on how the specified project work should be done. In high-value procurement contracts, the project manager may host a bidders' conference in which all potential suppliers meet with the project manager or board and ask questions concerning the specification, thus ensuring that they all have the same information on which to base prices and proposals.

The contract type might also be negotiated, but usually the type of work or goods being procured dictates the appropriate contract type. Table 6.5 lists the most common contract types and their attributes.

Most large partner organisations (for instance, local authority library or cultural services, academic institutions)

Table 6.5 **Common contract types**

Contract type	Description	Risk
Fixed fee	Fixed fee for the goods or services provided. The simplest form of a fixed price contract is a purchase order for a specified item to be delivered by a specified date for a specified price.	The supplier has the risk of cost overruns.
Time and materials	The contractor pays for the time and materials to complete the work.	Low risk as long as the contract includes a 'not to exceed' clause as a price cap.
Unit price	Fee per item or hour purchased.	Low risk.
Incentive fee contracts	These contracts award a bonus if the project work is done early and can include penalties if the work is late or lacking in quality.	Usually low risk.

use standard contracts, standard descriptions of procurement items, non-disclosure agreements, proposal evaluation criteria checklists, or standardised versions of all parts of the needed bid documents. The project manager can make good use of these standardised documents and ensure that contractual arrangements are approved by the appropriate administrative or management staff in the lead project organisation.

European Union procurement rules

Project managers in the European Union should be aware of the requirements of the EU directives on procurement, last revised in January 2008 and reviewed bi-annually.[6]

The directives cover supplies, services and works, and the current financial thresholds, above which it is mandatory for any public sector organisation to procure using the EU procedures, are based on a value or likely spend for the specified requirement over 4 years or 48 months:

- Supplies: £139,893
- Services: £139,893
- Works: £3,497,313

To work out whether or not a project tender falls within the directives the project manager can

- multiply an annual cost by 4;
- multiply a monthly cost by 48.

When undertaking initial scoping of likely spend, it is recommended that some leeway on value is given of perhaps 10 per cent to minimise the risk of actual spending exceeding the threshold. If an extension period is allowed for within the terms of the contract this should also be a consideration when calculating the total potential contract value.

There are four procedures for tendering under the EU rules:

- *Open*: anybody who responds *must* be invited to tender. This is used where there are a limited number of suppliers or the project manager does not know the market they are dealing with.
- *Restricted*: those invited to bid can be restricted to between 5 and 20. This is used where there are many suppliers and the project manager wishes to restrict the number of companies invited to tender.
- *Negotiated*: this procedure is used where there are a very limited number of suppliers for the product or service, for instance in the case of some software packages.

- *Accelerated*: allows access to greatly reduced timescales. This is used when something happens beyond the control of the project organisation, such as a fire.

Project managers need to bear in mind when planning project procurement that an EU tender can take up to six months from start to finish, and no procedure, other than the accelerated procedure, takes less than six to seven weeks from publishing the procurement notice to award of contract.

Selecting subcontractors and suppliers

Many factors can be evaluated in the selection decision process and the project manager will be responsible for determining the evaluation criteria. The primary determinant for an off-the-shelf item can be the price or cost, but if the supplier proves unable to deliver the products, services or results in a timely manner, the lowest proposed price may not be the lowest cost.

Two techniques for selecting winning bids are:

- Weighting systems – the method used to minimise the effect of personal prejudice on selection. Most such systems involve assigning a numerical weight to each of the evaluation criteria, rating the bids or proposals on each criterion, multiplying the weight by the rating and totalling the resulting figures to arrive at an overall score.
- Independent estimates – sometimes referred to as a 'should-cost' estimate which the project partner organisations can either prepare or have an independent estimate of the costs as a basis for proposed pricing. Significant differences from these should-cost estimates or budget ceilings can be an indication that the specification of work or terms of reference were not adequate, that the bidders either

misunderstood or failed to respond fully to the specification or that the marketplace changed.

Contract negotiation

In order to reach a mutual agreement prior to signing the contract, the structure and requirements of the contract are clarified in contract negotiation. The final contract language should reflect all the agreements reached. Subjects covered may include responsibilities and authorities, applicable terms and law, technical and business management approaches, proprietary rights, contract financing, technical solution, overall schedule payments and price. For complex procurement items contract negotiation can be an independent process with inputs (e.g. an issues or 'open items' list) and outputs (e.g. documented decisions) of its own. For simple procurement items, the terms and conditions of the contract can be fixed and non-negotiable and only need to be accepted by the selected supplier.

It is quite common for the project manager not to be the lead negotiator on the contract though they and other members of the project team should be available during negotiations to provide any clarification of the technical quality and management requirements.

Monitoring subcontractors' performance

Consultancy services subcontracted within projects are very often poorly monitored for performance. In any substantial assignment there should be provision for the consultants to report on the status of their work at reasonable intervals. The best way to do this is to hold fairly frequent progress meetings with the consultant or their team leader at which they present a verbal status report and a short written summary. Phased payments are usually linked to these progress meetings.

In short-term assignments (between one and four months, for instance) interim reports may not be feasible, but even then it is sensible for the project manager or a member of the project team to see a draft report and discuss it with the consultants before the final report is completed. This is an opportunity to review data and to bring out into the open any assumptions which need to be made explicit.

Notes

1. See JISC infoNet guidelines on project management. Online at: *http://www.jiscinfonet.ac.uk/infokits/project-management.*
2. Adapted from ibid.
3. From Joint Costing and Pricing Steering Group (JISC) Consolidated TRAC Guidance. Online at: *http://www.jcpsg.ac.uk/guidance/about.htm.*
4. From guidelines produced by the JISC for academic institutions. Online at: *http://www.jisc.ac.uk/fundingopportunities/bidguide/fulleconomiccosting.aspx.*
5. Joseph Phillips. *Real World Project Management: Procurement Management*. Online at: *http://www.projectsmart.co.uk/pdf/procurement-management.pdf.*
6. A useful UK government guide can be found at: *http://www.ogc.gov.uk/documents/Introduction_to_the_EU_rules.pdf.*

7

Evaluation and review

Introduction

Before considering evaluation and review in a project management context, it is useful to revisit where monitoring, evaluation and impact assessment may begin and end in relation to projects. Figure 7.1 shows the results chain in any project from intervention to effects. Project monitoring is primarily concerned with the details of the intervention itself (what was done), while evaluation (and review) focuses on its effects.

Figure 7.1 **The results chain**

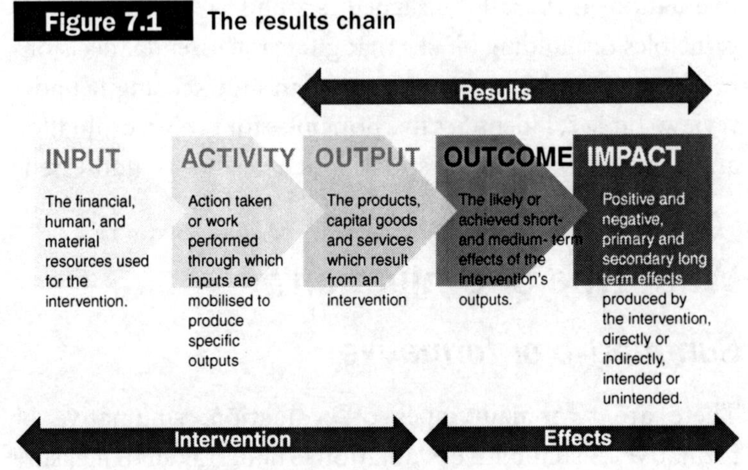

Planning evaluations

An evaluation plan (often called a monitoring and evaluation or M&E Plan) should be drawn up and costed as part of the detailed project plan and budget. If monitoring, evaluation and review are not fully integrated into a project plan, it is virtually impossible to undertake effective and meaningful evaluation at the end of the project because the relevant information and data, upon which evaluation depends, will not have been collected in usable ways. Figure 7.2 provides an example of an M&E Plan matrix from a development project context, in which a logical framework is the key planning document.

The key elements of the evaluation plan will cover:

- the general principles for monitoring, evaluation and review;
- what type of evaluations or reviews will take place;
- who will carry out the evaluations;
- the design of the evaluation (research methods, sample etc.).

General principles for evaluation

Evaluation is usually designed around a set of general principles or building blocks that guide the essential decisions in putting together an evaluation plan and keeping it under review. Table 7.1 identifies five principles for project evaluation and some of the main questions which need to be addressed.

What type of evaluation?

Summative or formative

There are two main types of evaluation: summative or formative. A summative evaluation is undertaken to measure

Figure 7.2 Logical framework matrix of Monitoring & Evaluation Plan

Overall objectives	Beneficiaries actually benefit	Confidence between partners, donors and stakeholders enhanced

Project purpose	Ensured quality of implementation of the project

Results	Legal basis assured (why?)		Clear project design (what to monitor)		Logistics of M&E assured (how to organise)				Information made available (how to disseminate)					Adjustments made to the project design
	Mandate for decision making achieved	Ownership/ partnership of the M&E process ensured	Project design clear to all stakeholders	Indicators set up	Workplan for monitoring accepted	Job allocated to competent monitors	Timely and right information collected	Adequate funding for M&E allocated	Data identified and collected	Informaiton analysed	Clear information flow established	Report and recommen-dations delivered	Vibrant presentations of findings made	Feedback from outside received
Solutions	Approve job descriptions of project managers	Ownership achieved	Project (objectives) designed in relevance with problems of beneficiaries	Indicators designed at the very beginning	Monitoring should be carefully planned including time frame	Monitors understand thoroughly about the project objectives	Information needs assessed	Budget for M&E included in the project documents	Inventories data availabili-ties (data banks other institutions / projects)	Computerised system set up	Information flows through management levels	'One-page report' principle used	Nicely formatted and readable publications made to the public	Feedback system set up at the beginning
	Clear mandate of monitoring authority	Partnership obtained	Context analysis with culture, gender, ethnics aspects	Indicators identified with local cultural and social perceptions	Evaluation is missions, monitoring is continuously based/routines	Monitors are trained with monitoring skills	Relevant methods of data collection applied		Select data collection techniques/ methods	Data are aggregated and analysed	Reports sent to upper level duly and timely	Format for reporting system established	Recommendations and lessons learnt disseminated	Feedback and recommendations used to readjust the plan
	Decision making mandate is clear	Transparency gained		Indicators defined with discussions with beneficiaries and partners	Information assessment done	Clear assignment delegated to monitors	Frequency and time schedule for data collection identified		Train data collectors / interviewers	Manage by the organization or by outside analysts	Transparency in communication built up	Filing/reference system set up		Feedback mechanism applied as a routine in management process
		Stakeholders involved		Baseline study included in the beginning										Reference/share of findings with similar projects
		Monitoring by local partners (GLOS) via consultative committee		Use focus groups for qualitative indicators										Headquarter needs to monitor the progress of the monitoring
		Evaluation to be done by/in consideration of beneficiaries												

Table 7.1 **Evaluation elements**[1]

Purposes of evaluation or review	What is the main purpose of the evaluation or review? What is the main focus of the evaluation? Do you want to focus on the process of implementation (the way the project is organised) or on the outcomes that are achieved, or both? For instance, is the evaluation primarily intended: ■ to improve performance by helping project partners manage the project? ■ to provide evidence as to the usability, cost-effectiveness and added value of the systems, services, products etc. that are being developed? ■ to contribute to the overall learning in a programme of change as a whole that will be useful for future projects and programmes?
Stakeholders	Who are the different actors who have a stake in the project evaluation? For instance, ■ project decision-makers; ■ people whose support and cooperation is necessary for the project to succeed; ■ people who are expected to use or to act on the evaluation findings.
Utilisation	What resources are available for the evaluation? How will the evaluation be integrated into the project? How will the evaluation, for instance, ■ involve stakeholders in ways that will increase their commitment to acting on the findings? ■ involve users and beneficiaries so as to increase the prospects for uptake and diffusion of project outcomes? How will the learning from the project be captured and made available for other and future projects and planning?
User or beneficiary involvement	How will users or end beneficiaries be involved in the evaluation? For instance, ■ which users need to be involved? ■ how should they be selected? ■ when and how often is data or feedback to be gathered? ■ how will their motivation be sustained?
Methods and techniques	What kinds of evaluation questions will be asked and what research methods are appropriate? For instance, ■ when and how often will the data be collected? ■ what methods will be used to collect the data?

the result of a project. It is a verdict on whether or not the project succeeded and it focuses on capturing data, drawing conclusions and presenting a final report. A summative evaluation is often used by externally funded projects as an audit to inspect and check that everything has been done right and in accordance with the terms of reference.

PRINCE2 follows the summative route, regarding evaluation as part of 'Closing the Project' using an internal evaluation that has the following objectives:

- Update the project plan with actual activities from the final stage.
- Assess the results of the project against what it was intended to achieve.
- Examine the records of the completed project to assess the quality of its management, especially quality and risk management.
- Identify lessons to be learned from the project and applied on future projects.

A formative evaluation may be iterative and certainly starts much earlier in the life of a project. It is often allied to monitoring and provides the feedback loop to guide project change during its implementation. It collects data and offers options based on the analysis of the required data and focuses more on understanding and learning by providing various short reports at appropriate times. Midterm reviews of programmes and larger projects have many of the characteristics of a formative evaluation.

Not all projects need to be evaluated. Typically there are four points at which evaluation may take place: rolling; midterm; end of project; and/or post project.

- *Rolling evaluations (formative)* tend to be used when there is a clear aim to test the innovative nature of a project, or a particular intervention within a project (for instance, the efficacy of a training programme; the success or otherwise of a museum education summer school), for its ability to be mainstreamed or scaled up. Rolling evaluations concentrate on in-depth monitoring data and drawing regular conclusions. The lessons learnt from this should then inform and, if necessary, lead to the recommendation of change to certain practices.

- *Midterm evaluations or reviews (formative)* are undertaken to enable management to obtain an independent assessment of the progress so far when the project period is usually over two years in length. Midterm evaluations or reviews concentrate mainly on the outputs and their contribution to achieving the project purpose. They also include an assessment of the budget and actual expenditure and the project management's capacity to keep to the planned targets. The results of midterm evaluations should be used to assist the project manager in understanding what is going on and what needs to be done in the future.
- *End-of-project evaluations or reviews (summative)* are useful in assessing the efficiency of the management and its effectiveness in delivering outputs on time and within budget. They are also used to audit the finance; end-of-project financial information can help funders to make decisions as to whether they should provide further support. End-of-project evaluations are also able to gauge the level of project success and identify lessons learnt for future actions.
- *Post project evaluations (summative)* concentrate on the level of sustainable project outcomes being utilised by users and end beneficiaries and can also be very useful in evaluating the sustainability and scalability of projects. Particularly in projects in education, information delivery and cultural heritage, the benefits and impact of a project may take some

time to be realised and it is important not to undertake the evaluation too early. The evaluation should be planned to coincide with the time the project impact is expected to be felt, sometimes a year or more after the project is completed.

Review or evaluation

The terms 'review' and 'evaluation' are often used interchangeably, but they can be subtly different in scope and purpose. Table 7.2 presents one view of the scope of and relationships between monitoring, reviewing and evaluation, as a guide to determining the required approach.

Who will carry out the evaluation?

This question very much depends upon the size, scope and complexity of the project.

The evaluation may require additional staff for data collection and analysis. At the planning stage it should be decided whether the planned evaluation(s) can be conducted internally (from within a project partner organisation) or whether external expertise will be needed. Barbara Allan[2] provides a useful comparison of the advantages and disadvantages of various options: see Table 7.3.

Designing the evaluation

Evaluation frameworks

An evaluation framework can be used as a way of determining the different elements that should be included in the evaluation, and the relationship between them. The elements of a typical evaluation framework are shown in Figure 7.3.

Table 7.2 **Comparisons between monitoring, reviewing and evaluation**

	Monitoring	Reviewing	Evaluation
When is it done?	Continuously – throughout the life of the project	Occasionally – in the middle or at the end of the project	Occasionally – in the middle or at the end of the project
What is measured?	Efficiency – use of inputs, activities, outputs, assumptions	Effectiveness, relevance and immediate effects – progress in or achievement of purpose	Longer-term effects, impact and sustainability – achievement of purpose and goals, and unplanned change
Who is involved?	Project staff within the project organisation(s)	Project staff, internal stakeholders from the project organisation(s)	Internal stakeholders, external stakeholders and project beneficiaries
What sources of information are used?	Internal project documents	Internal project documents and other documentation from project organisation(s)	Internal project documents and other documentation from project and external stakeholder organisation(s)
Who uses the results?	Project manager and project staff	Project manager, senior managers in project organisation(s), funders and beneficiaries	Project manager, senior managers in project organisation(s), funders and beneficiaries
How are the results used?	To make minor changes	Changes in project directions, organisational strategy and future work	Major changes in project or programme directions, organisational policy, strategy and future work

Table 7.3 **Who should carry out the evaluation? (adapted from Barbara Allan, 2004)**

	Advantages	**Disadvantages**
Project manager or someone from project team	Knows the project and its processes Knows the stakeholders Carries out the evaluation as part of their project work	May be biased May not have very good evaluation skills
Colleague from a project partner organisation	Understands the context Carries out the evaluation as part of their 'normal' work and doesn't require additional payment Enables them to learn more about the project	May be biased May not have very good evaluation skills
Colleague from partner organisation with specialist role e.g. researcher, evaluator, quality assurance	Understands the context Has very good evaluation skills Carries out the evaluation as part of their 'normal' work and doesn't require additional payment Enables them to learn more about the project	May be biased
Consultant or external researcher	Has very good evaluation skills Unbiased Takes additional time to understand the project and its context Ideally has experience of evaluating a wide range of projects and can bring a broader perspective	Takes time to identify appropriate person and ensure they have relevant skills May be relatively expensive as needs to be paid in 'real money' May not understand specific context
Funding organisation or their representative	May have very good evaluation skills Will bring in an external perspective and experience of evaluating a wide range of projects	May not have very good evaluation skills May focus on a fixed or limited set of evaluation criteria May not understand the specific context or project

Figure 7.3 **Overview of elements in a typical evaluation framework**

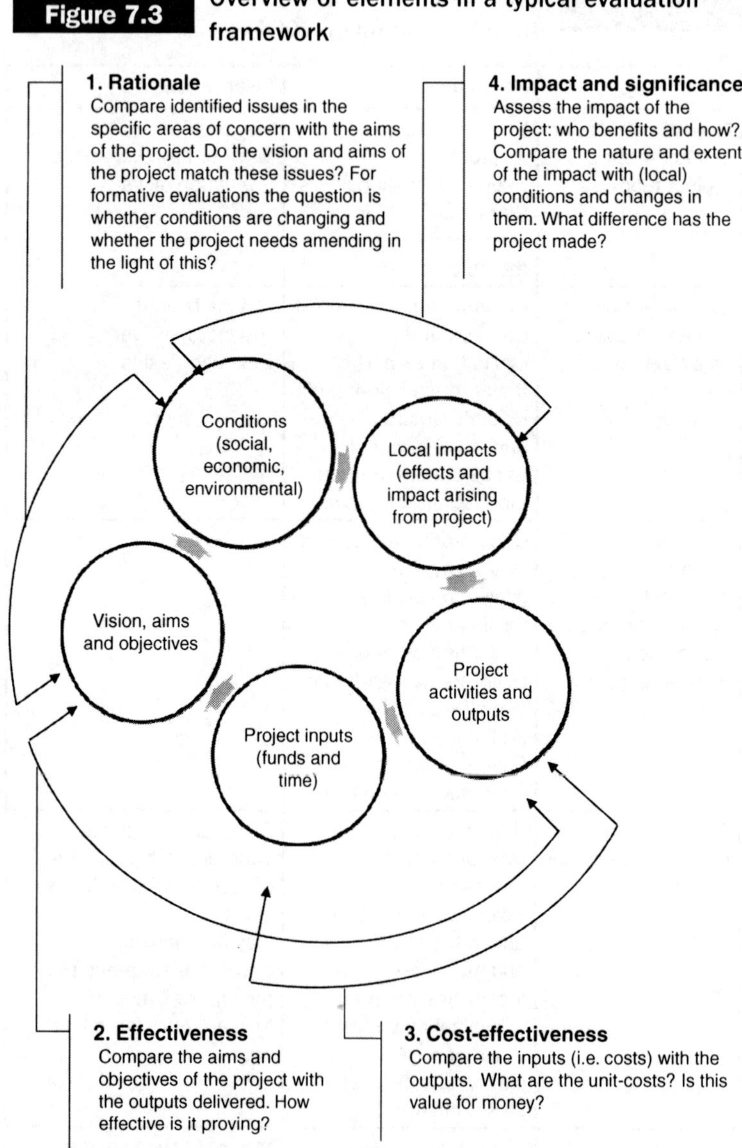

When specifying the terms of reference for an evaluation or review the project manager should give consideration to the elements in the evaluation framework appropriate to the context and nature of the project. These considerations may be heavily influenced, or even pre-determined, by the requirements of the project funder.

For instance, if the project is funded in part or as a whole by any development agency – multilateral (e.g. the World Bank, EuropeAid) or bilateral (e.g. UK Department for International Development) – then evaluations will almost certainly be required to adopt the evaluation criteria of the OECD's Development Assistance Committee (Table 7.4) as the basis of the evaluation framework.

Evaluation approaches

There are several different approaches to evaluation, with different strengths and weaknesses, appropriate for different projects and project contexts. While it is unlikely to be the project manager who undertakes the final design and implementation of the evaluation, it is important to understand the range of options open and, if appropriate, to specify the use of a particular approach in the terms of reference. Five different approaches are described briefly below and more detailed sources of guidance on each are provided in the useful resources section at the end of the book.

Results-based project monitoring and evaluation

This is probably the most familiar approach to monitoring and evaluation, dependent upon results-based management that relies on causality and attribution with changes shown in the form of a chain or framework; for example activities to outputs to outcomes to impact (see Figure 7.1). A number of tools or logic models have been developed for results-based

Table 7.4 The OECD Development Assistance Committee (DAC) evaluation criteria

Relevance	The appropriateness of project objectives to the problems that the project is supposed to address, and to the physical and policy environment within which it operates, including an assessment of the logic and completeness of the project planning process, and the internal logic and coherence of the project design.
Efficiency	The fact that the project results have been achieved at reasonable cost, i.e. how well inputs have been converted into results, in terms of quality, quantity and time, and the quality of the results achieved.
Effectiveness	An assessment of the contribution made by project results to achievement of the project purpose, and how assumptions have affected project achievements.
Impact	The effect of the project on its wider environment, its contribution to the wider programme or sectoral objectives summarised in the project's overall objectives, and on achievement of the overarching policy objectives of the funding organisation.
Sustainability	An assessment of the likelihood of benefits produced by the project to continue to flow after external funding has ended, and with particular reference to factors of ownership by beneficiaries, policy support, economic and financial factors, socio-cultural aspects, gender equality, appropriate technology, environmental aspects, and institutional and management capacity.

management in projects, but the logical framework approach has become the most widely used, particularly in EU funded programmes and in development work.

Results-based monitoring and evaluation mean

- clearly identifying project beneficiaries', and other stakeholders', problems and opportunities;
- setting clear and agreed objectives, targets and milestones;

- monitoring progress towards results, and resources consumed, with the use of appropriate indicators;
- identifying and managing assumptions/risks, while bearing in mind expected results and the necessary resources;
- using quantifiable indicators and qualitative narratives to measure progress;
- increasing knowledge by learning lessons and integrating them into decisions;
- changing objectives as a consequence of learned lessons;
- reporting on results achieved and the resources involved.

Social return on investment (SROI)

SROI is an approach to evaluation that was developed during the last decade by the New Economics Foundation (in the UK) with the needs of the 'third sector' (community and voluntary organisations and non-governmental organisations using government or development funding to effect social and cultural change). SROI is intended to incorporate the social, environmental and economic impacts of projects across a range of stakeholders, and more accurately reflect the value that organisations are achieving through their projects, which is not necessarily quantifiable in concrete results, efficiency gains or income generated.

> Essentially, SROI encourages a new way of thinking about value and enables a mode of decision-making that is informed by the things that matter to people and communities. In this sense, it should not be seen as a mechanistic process, or one that requires the support of ongoing expert opinion. Instead, SROI promotes the philosophy that measurement systems should be

> embedded within an organisation, that they should inform strategic planning, and that those delivering services are often best placed to engage with their stakeholders and respond to new information.[3]

SROI approaches have much to offer projects in libraries and other cultural heritage organisations, in which typically the required outcomes and impact of the project are of an 'intangible' and social nature. This is acknowledged in recent work for the UK Department of Culture, Media and Sport by BOP Consulting, in which they note that 'evidence regarding libraries' impact should not claim one-to-one causative relationships, but should concentrate instead on showing how libraries can "make a contribution towards"/"have a bearing on" a range of socio-economic priorities.'[4] The report suggests a logic chain for capturing the impacts of public libraries in England through evaluation, which includes the use of SROI approaches (Figure 7.4).

Figure 7.4 Data framework for the logic chain for capturing the impacts of public libraries in England

Logic Model Stage	SERVICES, ACTIVITIES & RESOURCES	INTRINSIC BENEFITS	EXTRINSIC BENEFITS: INTERMEDIATE OUTCOMES	EXTRINSIC BENEFITS: LONG TERM OUTCOMES
Focus of data & evidence capture	Service inputs and outputs	Immediate impact of the outputs		Long term impact & value
Main types of indicators	▪ No. of users, participants, lenders ▪ Demographics of participants, lenders ▪ Costs of delivery ▪ Partnerships established	▪ Achievement indicators showing goal conversion, distance travelled, progression outcomes ▪ Attitudinal data on changes to perceptions and values, changes to behaviour and intentions to act ▪ Attitudinal data on perceptions of value, utility and quality of delivery		▪ Statistical correlations ▪ Cost-benefit/ROI ratios ▪ Opportunity costs ▪ Longitudinal data
Main data capture & research methods	▪ Management information systems ▪ Surveys of users and intermediaries	▪ Surveys of users and intermediaries ▪ Stakeholder testimony and surveys		▪ Statistical analysis (e.g. regression, multi-level modelling) ▪ Economic modelling (ROI/SROI) ▪ RCT/experimental design ▪ Network analysis/modelling

◄——————► STAKEHOLDERS' MAIN INTERESTS

Source: BOP (2009)

Utilisation-focused evaluation (UFE)

UFE is based on the principle that an evaluation should be judged by its utility and that no matter how methodologically sound, an evaluation is not truly a good evaluation unless the findings are used. 'Use' is concerned with how real people in the real world might apply the evaluation findings and experience the evaluation process. UFE does not depend upon any particular evaluation content, model, method or theory. Rather, it is a process for helping the primary intended users select the most appropriate content, model, methods, theory, and uses of evaluation for their particular situation.

From a project manager's perspective the UFE approach advocates:

- the inclusion of key project partners and stakeholders in writing the terms of reference for the evaluation;
- the creation of an evaluation resource group to oversee the progress of the evaluation and use of its findings;
- the use of an external and expert evaluator; and
- building in to the evaluation process sufficient time for detailed stakeholder feedback, to ensure their ownership of the evaluation findings, checking for factual errors and for the evaluators to step back and reflect.

All of these factors make UFE a challenging approach to adopt in small project contexts, but one which has much to offer if project managers are committed to making the evaluation and review of projects and project activities formative and valuable. UFE approaches are particularly valuable if the subject of evaluation is, for instance, a new library service or museum offer targeting specific communities or population groups, which depend upon the influence and ownership of end-user stakeholders.

Participatory monitoring and evaluation (PME)

In a development project context, the UK's DFID advocates a self-evaluation approach called 'participatory monitoring and evaluation'. PME has similarities with UFE in that local stakeholders in the evaluation influence decisions about evaluation processes and the evaluation activities build local capacity for learning and collective action. PME approaches also encompass a range of evaluation tools and methodologies, adapted to fit a particular project context. It specifically precludes, however, the use of external expertise in carrying out evaluations.

PME is recognised for its potential to

- build partnerships and sense of local ownership over projects;
- build consensus among project staff and partners about goals and objectives;
- enhance local learning, management capacity and skills;
- provide timely, reliable, and valid information for management decision-making;
- increase cost-effectiveness of monitoring and evaluation information;
- empower local people to make their own decisions about the future.

Most significant change (MSC)

The most significant change (MSC) technique is also a form of participatory monitoring and evaluation, conceived in a development project context but also increasingly drawn upon in community, voluntary and public sector projects. In this

Table 7.5 **Summary of the differences between conventional and participatory evaluation approaches[5]**

Conventional evaluation	Participatory evaluation
Why	
Accountability, usually summary judgements about the project to determine if funding continues	To empower local people to initiate, control and take corrective action
Who	
External experts	Community members, project staff, facilitator
What	
Predetermined indicators of success, principally cost and production output; assesses project impact	People identify their own indicators of success
How	
Focus on 'scientific objectivity' distancing of evaluators from other participants; uniform complex procedures; delayed limited access to results	Self-evaluation; simple methods adapted to local culture; open immediate sharing of results through local involvement in evaluation processes
When	
Midterm and completion Sometimes ex-post	Any assessment for programme improvement; merging of monitoring and evaluation, hence frequent small evaluations.

approach, many project stakeholders are involved both in deciding the sorts of change to be recorded and in analysing the data. As a form of monitoring it occurs throughout the project cycle and provides project management information. As an evaluation technique it focuses on project outcomes and impact.

MSC does not make use of pre-defined indicators, especially ones that have to be counted and measured. Answers to the central evaluative questions about change are often in the form of stories of who did what, when and why, and the reasons why the event was important.

> Essentially, the process involves the collection of significant change stories emanating from the field level, and the systematic selection of the most significant of these stories by panels of designated stakeholders or staff. The designated staff and stakeholders are initially involved by 'searching' for project impact. Once changes have been captured, various people sit down together, read the stories aloud and have regular and often in-depth discussions about the value of these reported changes. When the technique is implemented successfully, whole teams of people begin to focus their attention on program impact.[6]

Evaluation research methods

The selection of research methods in an evaluation is shaped by what the evaluation is for, what kinds of questions are being asked, who the users or audiences of the evaluation are and what views they have about what constitutes valid and reliable data. Other considerations to take into account include the available resources for evaluation, logistical aspects (such as location of service points, geographical spread of end beneficiaries), as well as the expertise and methodological preferences of evaluators.

In most project evaluations a mix of quantitative (e.g. questionnaire surveys, gathering statistical data from monitoring exercises) and qualitative (e.g. focus groups, interviews, observation) methods are used. The mix allows the evaluator to gather evidence about performance indicators in different ways, to 'triangulate' or validate different assessment findings. Table 7.6 suggests when quantitative and qualitative approaches are appropriate in relation to project indicators.

Table 7.6 **Quantitative and qualitative evaluation methods**

	Outputs (monitoring)	**Outcomes (evaluation)**	**Impact (impact assessment)**
Quantitative methods	What outputs? How many? How long? Where? When?	Take-up and use of outputs among target groups Geographical distribution/ spread of use	What happened? (quantifiable 'surrogates' or 'proxy' indicators)
Qualitative methods	Awareness of outputs among target groups Opinions about outputs among target groups	What outcomes? Quality of outcomes Who has been affected? How have they been affected?	What kinds of impact? Impact upon whom? How has the impact manifested itself?

Quantitative data

In general, quantitative data is analysed to look for patterns and trends. For example:

- *Frequencies:* to establish how many of something there are. For example, how many schoolchildren attended a museum education event?

- *Proportions:* to look at what percentage of the total is in each category. For example, what percentage of those schoolchildren fell into age group categories x, y and z?
- *Cross-tabulation:* to establish whether two things are associated. For example, were schoolchildren from one particular area more likely to attend the event than those from another area?
- *Trend:* to examine the change over time in numbers, proportions or rates. For example, how do the numbers of schoolchildren attending the event this year compare with those last year?
- *Rates:* how many incidents there are per so many people in the population. For example, out of the total school age population within the museum's target area, how many children attended the event?

Qualitative data

In general, analysing qualitative data is not about counting; it is about identifying themes and underlying factors and exploring how and why things happen. For example, by:

- *Defining ideas:* establishing what people mean by a term or phrase. For example, how do respondents define 'improved library service'?
- *Generating types or categories:* creating categories for respondents' perceptions/attitudes/experiences. For example, what characteristics emerge from different respondents' views on improved library services (positive/negative/mixed views)?
- *Examining 'processes':* looking at how and why things are done in one way and exploring the alternatives. For example, examining the way in which the new

processes for digitisation of collections impact upon the organisation(s) and exploring the alternatives.

- *Generating explanations:* using the data to help explain why or how something happens.

Managing the evaluation process

Main project management tasks

Managing an evaluation exercise usually involves the following major tasks for the project manager:

- establishing the need for an evaluation within the parameters of the project plan;
- scoping the evaluation, including specifying the terms of reference;
- drafting tender documents for the evaluation study and selecting the contractor according to the requisite procurement rules;
- briefing the contractor and the stakeholders involved;
- supporting the evaluator(s) through provision of documentation, facilitation of meetings with project staff and stakeholders, etc.;
- ensuring the production of a high-quality evaluation report and the dissemination of evaluation findings and recommendations;
- supporting the use of evaluation findings and managing the implementation of recommended changes in project process or plans.

Evaluation outcomes and dissemination

Depending on the focus, the expected outcome of a formative evaluation (for instance, a mid-term evaluation) is a decision taken to

- continue project implementation as planned;
- re-orient the project in some way; or
- stop the project in the worst case.

End-of-project or ex post evaluations are normally concerned with the question whether or not, in future, similar projects should be initiated, and how to consider the outcomes of the evaluation in the definition of organisational policies, cooperation strategies, and subsequent programming.

Evaluations are useless unless they are used. The following key issues should be considered to ensure good feedback and subsequent use and integration of evaluation findings in future project implementation, programming or policy change:

- Evaluation as a consultative process: ensuring the participation of relevant stakeholders, enhancing ownership of the evaluation and its results.
- Project managers are responsible for keeping the project board, partners and other closely involved stakeholders appropriately informed on progress at each key stage of the evaluation.
- The evaluation results need to be disseminated e.g. through seminars or workshops, publications and media.
- Good feedback mechanisms will help to assure quality in evaluations and ensure that findings are taken into account in subsequent project proposals.

Notes

1. Adapted from *Evaluation of the Electronic Libraries Programme: Guidelines for eLib Project Evaluation*, prepared by John Kelleher, Elizabeth Sommerland and Elliot Stern. Tavistock Institute, 1996. Online at: *http://www.ukoln.ac.uk/services/elib/papers/tavistock/evaluation-guide/#general*.
2. Barbara Allan. *Project Management: Tools and Techniques for Today's ILS Professional*. London: Facet, 2004.
3. NEF. *Measuring Value: A Guide to Social Return on Investment (SROI)*, 2nd edn. London: NEF, 2008.
4. BOP Consulting. *Capturing the Impact of Libraries. Final Report*. London: DCMS, January 2009.
5. Taken from Phillip Dearden et al. *Tools for Development: A Handbook for Those Engaged in Development Activity*, Version 15.1. DFID, March 2003.
6. Rick Davies and Jess Dart. *The Most Significant Change (MSC) Technique: A Guide to Its Use*, Version 1.0. CARE International, 2005.

8

Quality management in projects

Introduction

Quality management as a concept and discipline emerged in the manufacturing sector and still mainly uses, often unhelpfully, the language of production. In general, as well as in project terms, it is 'the process of ensuring that the quality expected by the customer is achieved'.[1] The 'customer' is the recipient of the output(s), either internal or external to the organisation. Quality management concerns both product and process of production, in which:

- Product is any and all outputs *as perceived by the customer*: A product can be, for instance, a service, a training session, software, a website, or the helpfulness of enquiry desk staff in response to a problem.
- Process is everything carried out to generate the output including all the internal operations and sequences of operations used to generate and deliver the product to the customer for whom *perception is the reality*.

This emphasis on the customer's expectations and perception is the key to understanding quality management. In a project context, quality management is a process for ensuring that all project activities in the design, planning and implementation of a project are effective and efficient in meeting the project's objectives and, by implication therefore, the customer's expectations of the project outputs.

This chapter offers an overview of the main elements of project quality management and briefly explains the main concepts and terminology used in quality management where they are relevant to projects in libraries, archives and museums.

Quality management systems

The project stakeholder organisation or organisations may be an ISO 9000 or Investors in People accredited organisation or may have already in place other quality policies, supported by a quality management system (QMS). The QMS will be a set of standards covering all the normal work done by that organisation; each standard will cover the techniques, tools, required expertise and steps to be used in the creation of a specific type of product or service (for instance, if the product is a document the standard will cover its format and appearance).

A pre-existing QMS can be helpful in defining quality management procedures and responsibilities within a project (the quality plan), and certainly should be taken into account at the project planning and design stage. However, by its nature, a project is a temporary environment created for a particular purpose. As such, any required quality management for the project may take some elements from an appropriate QMS in place or the procedures may have to be created specifically for the project.

Challenges associated with project quality management

In libraries, museums and archive projects there are a number of typical challenges to overcome in ensuring adequate quality management:

- Relatively small or time-limited projects are common, in which quality management issues tend to be overlooked and quality planning may be considered to be implicit in the project plan itself.
- Project outputs tend to be services or products supported by services (for instance, a website offering access to collections and services): a typical QMS, or quality management guidelines, does not cover non-tangible outputs very helpfully.
- Where the 'customer' is the potential service user or community of interest, project organisations frequently have poor or unspecific information about the needs and requirements that the service is intended to address and the customers' expectations of project outputs; end-beneficiaries may be represented in the project by the stakeholder or partner organisations, which may have differing expectations and 'acceptance' criteria in mind and differing views of what their customers want.
- Project partner organisations are likely to take different approaches to quality management and use different QMS.
- Resources and budgets for project management, monitoring and evaluation – and by extension quality management – are likely to be restricted; this is an area where typically organisations try to save on project costs.

- Project staff are likely to lack familiarity with and experience in quality management and quality issues.

Project quality or deliverable quality?

Quality management can either focus on the quality of the project or on the quality of the deliverables. Project planners and managers need to decide where the balance should lie; quality managers checking project quality would look at completely different things than if they were looking at the quality of the outputs. The 'project quality' refers to process issues such as proper project management practices and managing change within the project. The output or 'deliverable' quality refers to whether the project outputs are 'fit for purpose' in relation to customer expectations and requirements. A good-quality project may deliver low-quality outputs, though it is more likely that a high-quality project will deliver high-quality outputs.

Managing quality and quality assurance

Assessing project performance in terms of time and cost is relatively easy but quality is harder to define and measure. A high-quality project may be one whose outputs

- meet the specification;
- meet stakeholder requirements.

Or alternatively one whose outputs

- are fit for purpose;
- satisfy the stakeholders.

What makes quality management challenging is that the chances of the initial specification being correct, or of the project stakeholders and beneficiaries being able adequately to articulate their real quality needs and expectations, are relatively slight, particularly where these relate to new and innovative services. Managing quality in library, museum and archival projects is likely to be about the project manager monitoring the project processes and procedures and aiming for outputs that are in line with the second definition above.

Quality assurance results from good quality management and is the provision of evidence to create confidence among all project stakeholders that quality-related activities are being performed effectively to ensure that a product or service will satisfy the stated quality requirements.

Quality assurance is concerned with both the 'deliverable quality' of the project (of its products and services) and the 'project quality' (its project management process and procedures). To be effective, therefore, quality assurance should be independent of the project itself and of the project manager. Many projects have some form of external quality assurance role built into the project structure. Such an assessor *evaluates* quality; the project manager is *responsible* for quality.

Essential components of quality management within projects

Quality management in projects is not a separate, independent process that occurs at the end of an activity to measure the level of quality of the output. It is – or should be – a continuous process, more about preventing and avoiding than measuring and fixing poor-quality outputs.

There are four essential components:

- Defining quality: establishing quality criteria or 'acceptance' criteria related to the project outputs. These should be established in the project plan, preferably, and they require real clarity from the project stakeholders, beneficiaries or 'customers'.
- A quality plan defines the use of any existing QMS, quality management responsibilities, etc.; this is especially important if the project has a consortium of partners.
- Quality controls of some sort, to monitor identified quality aspects of the project outputs.
- 'Acceptance' testing with (representatives of) the customer, piloting or testing critical project outputs.

Defining quality

It is very difficult, if not impossible, to achieve the business objectives or other benefits of a project's product or service if it does not meet the customer's quality expectations. But who is the customer in a service-oriented cultural heritage context?

In a development context, PM4DEV differentiates between project 'stakeholders' and 'beneficiaries' and suggests that

> quality management focuses on improving stakeholders' satisfaction through continuous and incremental improvements to processes, including removing unnecessary activities; it achieves that by the continuous improvement of the quality of material and services provided to the beneficiaries . . . The main principle of project quality management is to ensure the project will meet or exceed stakeholders' needs and expectations.

> The project team must develop a good relationship with key stakeholders, especially the donor and the beneficiaries of the project, to understand what quality means to them.[2]

This seems a useful approach to take in the cultural heritage sector, where project beneficiaries are likely to be represented, and their needs articulated, by stakeholder partner organisations.

Each project partner, and any external funder, will have certain required standards and expectations from the project, and of how the project delivers the expected benefits to the beneficiaries. The key question will be how far these standards and expectations reflect the real needs, interests and aspirations of the end-users or beneficiaries.

To be effective, quality definition should also come direct from the project beneficiaries. Whether mediated through project partners or gathered directly, enough must be understood by the project manager and project team about how beneficiaries define quality of project outputs from their perspective. If needs analysis research during the project planning stage is not adequate for this quality definition, the project manager should consider direct data collection using questions that seek to define what project success looks like from the beneficiary's perspective.

Quality characteristics and acceptance criteria

All processes, products or services (i.e. project outputs) have characteristics that can be used to define quality or 'acceptance' criteria. Quality characteristics relate to the attributes, measures and methods attached to that particular process, product or service – the priority given to different characteristics will depend upon how stakeholders and beneficiaries define quality. For instance, PM4DEV describes the quality characteristics associated with development assistance projects:

- Functionality is the degree by which equipment performs its intended function; this is important especially for clinical equipment – the operation should behave as expected.
- Performance is how well a product or service performs the beneficiaries' intended use. A water system should be designed to support extreme conditions and require little maintenance to reduce the cost to the community and increase its sustainability.
- Reliability: the ability of the service or product to perform as intended under normal conditions without unacceptable failures.
- Relevance: the characteristic of how a product or service meets the actual needs of the beneficiaries; it should be pertinent, applicable, and appropriate to its intended use or application.
- Timeliness: how the product or service is delivered in time to solve the problems when it's needed and not after.
- Suitability defines its fitness for use, it appropriateness and correctness; agricultural equipment must be designed to operate on the soil conditions the beneficiaries will use it on.
- Completeness: the service is complete and includes all the entire scope of expected services. Training sessions should be complete and include all the material needed to build a desired skill or knowledge.

- Consistency: services are delivered in the same way for every beneficiary.[3]

To use another example, in describing acceptance criteria JISC infoNet[4] cites a project to streamline a business process that has sub-products, such as a set of paper forms for capturing data, a computerised information system with requirements for each data entry screen and a set of report outputs. Acceptance or quality criteria for this project could include:

- target date
- functions required
- performance levels
- capacity
- downtime/availability
- running cost
- security levels
- level of skill required to operate.

Quality or acceptance criteria need to be defined for each phase of the project to allow the project manager to determine whether the outputs of each have been produced to an acceptable standard.

Quality planning

A project quality plan is an action plan defining a set of activities planned at the beginning of the project that will help to achieve quality in the project as it is implemented.

Producing a quality plan involves identifying all the outputs at the start of the project and deciding how to best validate their quality on the basis of the agreed quality or acceptance criteria. The quality plan identifies the mechanisms that should be in place to fix any quality problems uncovered, such as a follow-up process, the allocation of responsibilities to particular people and ensuring that changes are actually made. Time must be built into the project schedule for quality checking and for 'rework' following 'quality events'.

A quality plan needs to cover a number of elements:

- What needs to go through a quality check?
- What is the most appropriate way to check the quality?
- When should it be carried out?
- Who should be involved?
- What 'quality materials' should be used?

What needs to be checked?

Typically what need to be checked are the outputs. Any significant output from a project should have some form of quality check carried out.

What is the most appropriate way to check?

Quality checks should use the agreed quality or acceptance criteria for the project outputs. For instance, if a particular output should meet a technical standard then part of the quality checking should focus on compliance with the standard. If the output is a report of some kind then formatting, completeness, readability etc. may be criteria for checking.

When should it be carried out?

Most quality checks are undertaken through 'quality events', held just prior to the completion of the deliverable, though if there are long development lead times for a deliverable it might be sensible to hold earlier quality events. If, for example, the development of web pages for a particular project output will take ten weeks, it may be worth holding a quality check after four weeks to identify any problems early and reduce 'rework'.

Table 8.1 gives examples of 'quality events' that typically are used to review the quality of deliverables.

Who should be involved?

Primarily the project team members responsible for the output should be involved and other staff dependent on the

Table 8.1 **Examples of 'quality events'**

Quality events	Description
Expert review	Review of a deliverable by a person who is considered an expert in the area related to the deliverable.
Peer review	Review of deliverables by one's peers.
Multi-person review	Best undertaken when the purpose is to gain agreement between different stakeholders. Time should be allowed to reach agreement of conflicting opinions.
Walk-through	A walk-through is a useful technique to validate both the content and structure of a deliverable. Material should be circulated in advance.
Standard audit	A standard audit is carried out by a person who is only focused on ensuring the deliverable meets a particular standard(s).

type of quality event. Stakeholders and beneficiaries may be invited to take part in a quality review.

What quality materials should be used?

The materials used should be a prompt for the reviewers and quality checkers to ensure there are no gaps. Project managers may find it useful to reduce things like standards to checklists in order to make them more manageable.

Table 8.2 gives examples of 'quality materials' that might be used in a quality plan

Table 8.2 Examples of 'quality materials'

Quality materials	Description
Standards	Standards are instruction documents that detail how a particular aspect of the project must be undertaken. There can be no deviation from standards unless a formal variation process is undertaken
Guidelines	Unlike standards, guidelines are not compulsory. They are intended to guide a project rather than dictate how it must be undertaken.
Checklists	Checklists are lists that can be used as a prompt when undertaking a particular activity.
Templates	Templates are blank documents to be used in particular stages of a project. They will usually contain some examples and instructions.
Procedures	Procedures outline the steps that should be undertaken in a particular area of a project such as managing risks, or managing time.
Processes	A description of how something works, different to a procedure, which is a list of steps.

Quality control

Quality control is the use of techniques and activities that monitor specific project results to determine if they comply with relevant quality standards or criteria based on the project stakeholder and beneficiary expectations. Quality control as a process has one of three outcomes:

- *Acceptance:* the project stakeholders and/or beneficiaries accept or reject the product or service delivered. Acceptance usually occurs after the project output has been evaluated or tested in some way.
- *Rework:* the action taken to bring a rejected product or service into compliance with the quality requirements or stakeholder expectations. Rework can be expensive and costs associated with it may not be refundable by the project funder or from project partners.
- *Adjustments:* corrections or necessary steps required to prevent further quality problems or defects. Adjustments are made to the processes that produce project outputs.

Quality control tools

Here are some examples of quality control using specific problem-solving and monitoring methods and tools:

- cause and effect analysis
- Pareto analysis
- control charts
- controls database.

Cause and effect analysis

An Ishikawa or fishbone diagram provides a visual approach to analysing the cause and effects of problems; an example is shown in Chapter 4 (Figure 4.2).

Pareto analysis

This is based on the Pareto principle (also known as the 80/20 rule),[5] which assumes that most of the problems or results in any situation are determined by only a small number of causes. The chart helps to identify the vital few contributors that account for most quality problems. The chart is a form of histogram that orders any data gathered by frequency of occurrence, and shows, for instance, how many quality defects were generated by a particular type of identified cause. PM4DEV offers an example in which a Pareto chart is used to map errors in the collection of project beneficiary data.[6] The project team identified five categories of error and for each category counted the frequency of occurrence within the total number of errors. Figure 8.1

Figure 8.1 **Example of a Pareto chart used in quality control**

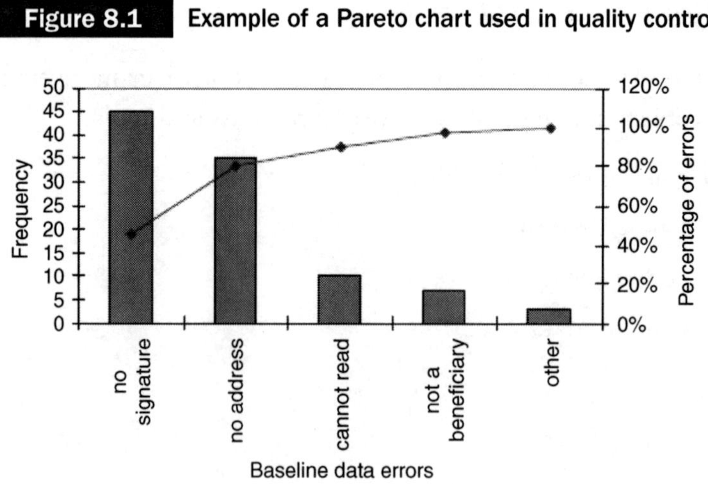

shows the resulting chart in which the bars represent each category of error. The chart reveals how 80 per cent of the errors could be reduced just by improving the collection of data in two categories.

Control charts

A control chart is a graphical display of data that illustrates the results of a process over time, the purpose being to prevent defects, rather than detect them or reject them. The chart reveals whether a process is in control or out of control over a specified length of time. Control charts are often used to monitor large-scale production. Figure 8.2 shows an example from PM4DEV of a control chart for the process of controlling the weight of products manufactured by development project beneficiaries for sale in international markets.

> The customer has a limit tolerance for defects; these are the upper and lower control limits in the chart. Random examination of the products provides data that once charted on the graph identifies the times when the

Figure 8.2 An example of a control chart from PM4DEV

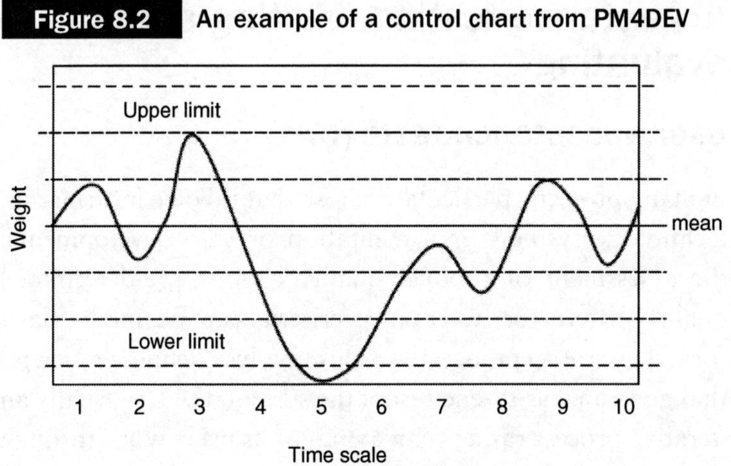

> production process created items that were outside the control limits, this helps the project determine actions to help the beneficiaries improve the quality of their work.[7]

Control charts can also be used, for instance, to monitor the volume and frequency of errors in documents, and to determine whether the cost or schedule variances are outside the acceptable limits set by the project board or funder.

Project controls database

A project controls database facilitates the recording of risks, issues and changes and helps with monitoring the progress of actions taken. The monitoring and control of quality can also be facilitated using a similar database tool. JISC infoNet designed a project controls database for use in Microsoft Access 2000 which is offered for download as an open source document, which can be adapted for use with a different database platform, or the User Guide can also be used as an outline specification for a similar database.[8]

Acceptance testing, piloting and evaluating

User acceptance tests (UAT)

In many projects, particularly those that involve information technology systems implementation or web developments, the assessment of product quality against pre-determined quality criteria or acceptance criteria can be made via a formal User Acceptance Test. This involves defining a 'script' that gives an end-to-end test of the system. UAT is usually an iterative process rather than a one-off as users work through the script and document any errors or issues. When all the issues are resolved the test is formally signed off.

JISC infoNet warns:

> Defined and measurable acceptance criteria and formal sign-off procedures, based on fitness for purpose, are important if you are to avoid the scope-creep associated with users trying to introduce 'nice-to-have' features at the last minute. Involvement in UAT also helps to give users a feeling of ownership and to manage their expectations of the project.[9]

The example (Table 8.3) of a quality plan for the PortCities digitisation project[10] shows incidences of UAT. The quality expectation was that the resulting project website would meet the 'lifelong learner' user needs. Testing was done with panels and focus groups of end-users or beneficiaries.

Piloting and evaluating products and services

Although information technologies play an increasingly important role in libraries, museums and archives, there are many projects where the customer-facing project outputs are not technology-based. The ultimate judge of quality remains the end-user or beneficiary, and project managers should always consider building in equivalents of the UAT to test whether or not the product or service being developed by the project meets beneficiaries' requirements and expectations. For instance, if a museum project's aim is to develop and produce a range of learner-focused resources based on collections, then the piloting of the content and design of these materials (whether or not they are to be ultimately

Table 8.3 **A digitisation project quality plan showing UAT events**

Area	Description	Project quality responsibility	Acceptance criteria
Technical	The New Opportunities Fund (NOF) technical standards will be adhered to and will form part of the Test Plan for the technical products. The exception to this is if this has been previously agreed by the NOF and the Consortium	Technical Team	Technical Test report. Sign-off by the Consortium Project Board (CPB)
Technical	User Acceptance Test (UAT) will be performed on the Content Management System (CMS)	Technical Team To set up the test environment and test scripts (this workload should form part of the service supplier contract with each Associate Partner) CPB organise the test subjects based on the target audience, including samples from the focus groups	UAT report. Sign-off by the CPB
Technical	User Acceptance Test (UAT) will be performed on the Templates	Technical Team To set up the test environment and test scripts (this workload should part of the service supplier contract with each Associate Partner) CPB will organise the test subjects based on the target audience, including sample from the focus groups	UAT report. Sign-off by the CPB

Project	All products defined will have a completed Product Description	Project Management Team	CPB sign-off
Content	All content will have the appropriate copyright clearance to be reproduced for the web and to be accessed by the general public	Associate Partner Project Managers	Criteria on content selection

delivered in digital or other forms) with a representative groups of users will be necessary at various stages in project implementation.

How a beneficiary defines quality may be completely subjective, but there are many ways to make quality objective: by defining the individual quality characteristics and determining one or more metrics that can be collected to mirror each required characteristic. These metrics or quality indicators can then be built into the project monitoring and evaluation procedures and research methods (see Chapter 7) to provide quality assurance and management information.

Notes

1. *Managing Successful Projects with TSO*, 2005.
2. PM4DEV. *Project Management Organizations: A Methodology to Projects for International Humanitarian Relief Organizations*. 2008. Online at: *http://www.pm4dev*.
3. Adapted from ibid.
4. JISC infoNet Project Management Toolkit. Online at: *http://www.jiscinfonet.ac.uk/infokits/project-management/managingquality*.

5. See useful Wikipedia explanation at: *http://en.wikipedia.org/wiki/Pareto_principle.*
6. PM4DEV, op. cit.
7. Ibid.
8. JISC infoNet. Online at: *http://www.jiscinfonet.ac.uk/infokits/projectmanagement/project-controls-database.*
9. JISC infoNet Project Management Toolkit. Online at: *http://www.jiscinfonet.ac.uk/infokits/project-management/managing quality*
10. PortCities was a digitisation project funded under the UK Lottery NOF – Digitise programme between 2004 and 2006. It was a partner consortium project led by the National Maritime Museum.

9

Sustainability of projects

Introduction

Sustainability has become an increasingly common preoccupation in the cultural heritage and academic sectors where innovation is so often fuelled by project funding. Sustainability relates to whether an innovative service or product can continue to be properly delivered and supported after the project has ended. Seen from an end-user perspective, sustainability is whether the flow of benefits will continue to be felt by project beneficiaries for a number of years after the project has been completed and project funding has ended. Sustainability does not necessarily mean the continuation of the project: the outcomes and benefits of the project may be sustainable even though the apparatus of the project has been dismantled.

Sustainability aspects

Prospects for sustainability should be a key factor in project planning, and measures to improve sustainability options (such as training and capacity development) might be included in project implementation.

Sustainability is commonly approached from four different aspects, depending upon the nature of the project, its context and partners:

- *Economic sustainability:* the affordability of the project elements and the ability of partner organisations to meet continuing operating, support and replacement costs at project end. In some contexts, the project may include the building of different channels of financing through community participation, which will tie economic sustainability closely to social and political sustainability.
- *Social sustainability:* the extent of target community involvement in the project planning and implementation and acceptance of outputs and services by end-users.
- *Political sustainability:* the necessary leadership and policy support and the success of change processes within the project organisations that might be necessary to embed project innovation. For instance, one of the biggest threats to ICT-enabled projects is resistance to change. If, for instance, staff in an organisation are reluctant to use new ICT-based management information systems in their work then the project's efforts to introduce them can hardly take off, much less be sustained over the long term.
- *Technological sustainability:* long-term effectiveness of any technology infrastructure introduced by the project, including the extent to which it provides the needed services and can be extended when required.

Particularly in a development or community regeneration context, sustainability can also be understood in terms of the capital assets available in the community targeted by the project: human capital (skills and expertise), financial capital, social capital (the strength of relationship networks and institutional forces), physical capital (equipment and infrastructure) and content capital (relevant knowledge and information assets, delivered appropriately).

Sustainability and quality

Quality and sustainability are closely related, the latter being in part dependent upon the former, and both being issues that must be addressed from the beginning of project design.

In the past it has been found that projects have failed to deliver sustainable benefits because they did not take sufficient account of a number of critical success factors, all of which are allied to, and often identical with quality concerns, such as:

- *Ownership by beneficiaries* – the extent to which target groups and beneficiaries of the project have participated and are involved in the project so that outputs will have their support after the end of project financing.
- *Policy support* – the quality of the relevant sector policy, and the extent to which the project partners (and other stakeholders such as government) have demonstrated political support for the continuation of project services beyond the period of direct support or external funding.
- *Appropriate technology* – whether the technologies applied by the project can continue to operate in the longer run (e.g. availability of spare parts and technical support; local capabilities for operation and maintenance).
- *Socio-cultural issues* – how the project takes into account local socio-cultural norms and attitudes, and what measures are taken to ensure that all beneficiary groups will have appropriate access to project services and benefits during and after implementation.
- *Institutional and management capacity* – the ability and commitment of the implementing partners to deliver the project and to continue to provide services beyond the period of funding.

- *Economic and financial viability* – whether the incremental benefits of the project outweigh its cost, and the project represents a viable long-term investment.

Sustainability and equity

Appropriate conditions for sustainability, especially financial sustainability, are often regarded as a pre-condition for deciding where to deploy project resources. A museum education project may select, for instance, schools with the best prospects for sustainability, as a way of getting a better return on investment. This approach can produce a policy dilemma. In many situations the external environment may be the limiting factor on sustainability, and individual institutions may be unable to meet sustainability criteria. This is a particular policy issue in development projects: some countries have large rural populations living in poverty. The low population density and lack of market indicate that if the projects are important that does not mean they are sustainable without external help.

Planning for sustainability

Planning for project sustainability can be expensive: it often involves prioritising long-term benefits over short-term savings. Some planning principles for promoting sustainability include:

- Plan and negotiate for financial sustainability from the start. In externally funded projects there is usually an expectation that there will be a transition from project funding to costs being covered by other sources, such as government or community funding or by revenue generation. Therefore, the contributions and expectations of all stakeholders, and appropriate timeframes within which financial alternatives might be put in place, should be defined clearly.

- Develop a clear funding strategy – who will meet which cost elements and how – and ensure that any assumptions about revenue generation are realistic.
- Choose appropriate information and other technologies that are stable and easy to support with affordable operating costs, avoiding vendor lock-in and high potential switching costs by adopting open standards from the start.
- Plan around cultural, educational or other sector goals rather than technology goals.

Table 9.1 **Checklist for assessing project sustainability**[1]

Ownership by beneficiaries	What evidence is there that all stakeholders and target groups support the project? How actively are they, and will they be, involved or consulted in project implementation? How far do they agree and commit themselves to achieve the objectives of the project?
Policy support	Is there a comprehensive, appropriate sector policy by the government? Is there evidence of sufficient support by responsible authorities to put in place the necessary supporting policies and resource allocations (human, financial, material) during and following implementation?
Appropriate technology	Is there sufficient evidence that the chosen technologies can be used at affordable cost and within the local conditions and capabilities of all types of users, during and after implementation?
Socio-cultural issues	Does the project take into account local socio-cultural norms and attitudes? Will the project promote a more equitable distribution of access and benefits?

(*Continued*)

Table 9.1 **Checklist for assessing project sustainability *(Cont'd)***

Institutional and management capacity	Is there sufficient evidence that the implementing partners will have the capacity and resources to manage the project effectively and to continue delivery of service into the longer term? If capacity is lacking what measures have been incorporated to build capacity during project implementation?
Economic and financial viability	Is there sufficient evidence that the benefits of the project justify the costs involved, and that the project represents the most viable way to addressing the needs of the target groups?

Revenue generation

In the UK cultural heritage and academic sectors, sustainability is more often than not interpreted to mean the necessity for revenue generation strategies to be in place and applicable at project end. Revenue generation options may range from, for instance, raising a proportion of required funds from the sale of parts or spin-offs of the project's products or services; charging for access to existing services; or launching the project product or service as a separate commercial or not-for-profit enterprise.

The consulting group Ithaka, in a study for the UK Strategic Content Alliance[1] which looked at the sustainability of 'online academic resources',[2] defines 'sustainability' as:

> 'having a mechanism in place for generating, or gaining access to, the economic resources necessary to keep the intellectual property or the service available on an ongoing basis'. This does not mean that every 'project' will need to launch an independent organisation to do this – indeed, most probably it should not. It also does not presuppose any particular method for revenue generation: an Open Access resource, for example, will have a different set of revenue options available to it than a project that is willing

> to charge a subscription fee, but both should be expected to develop a sustainable economic model. In short, every project needs to put in place an organisational infrastructure that includes focused leadership and an entrepreneurial culture that will enable it to continuously evaluate and select from a full range of strategic options available for revenue generation, management of expenses and opportunities for strategic collaboration. Pursuing sustainability is as much about a mindset and a process as it is about producing a written plan.

Their report includes a useful summary of the various revenue generation options for online resources and services, which is adapted in Table 9.2.

Table 9.2 **Summary of revenue generation options**

Model	Description	Success factors	Costs	Risks
Subscription	Access to at least part of content is restricted to subscribers	Meets needs of core audience that is significant in size Users willing to pay for content because of, e.g. uniqueness, timeliness, authenticity Adds value through aggregation that is difficult to replicate Users can afford to pay	Access controls Billing/ invoicing Sales function Subscriber retention Marketing	Limits potential usage and impact
Pay-per-use	Users can 'cherry pick' specific pieces of content or access	Users are willing to pay for discrete pieces of content Getting pricing right	Access controls Online transactions Marketing	Creating barrier to usage

(Continued)

Table 9.2 **Summary of revenue generation options (*cont'd*)**

Model	Description	Success factors	Costs	Risks
	resource for a short period of time	Search engine indexing Existence of large secondary audience		
Contributor pays	Content contributors pay to have their works or collections published online	Service offers benefits such as brand, audience, exposure, connection to related content Low cost	Sales function (to content contributors) May need to cover costs of reviewing content that is turned away Tools for ingesting content	As audience grows, costs increase rather than revenues (at least in short term) Difficult to build in funds for long term costs such as preservation and migration
Host institution support	Institution provides funds and in-kind contributions to support the project	Alignment with goals and mission of institution	Time to build relationships and make case for funding Political capital?	Institutional priorities may change Budgets can get cut
Corporate sponsorship	Non-profit website offers placement for corporate sponsor logo or other marketing feature in exchange for cash or in-kind contribution	Understanding interests of potential partners Resource has assets (audience, brand) that are valuable to partner Selecting partners with strong mission, audience, and/ or product fit Clear communication of goals and expectations	Business development time Legal costs of negotiating contracts	Can be complicated and time consuming to create and implement Any negative perceptions of the corporation can have repercussions for the service

Model	Description	Success factors	Costs	Risks
		Structure allows flexibility to change terms as environment evolves		
Advertising	Display ads are placed on pages throughout a website, in order to convey branding message or promote a product Search ads placed on the site generate revenue for the site publisher when a viewer clicks on them	High traffic and intensity of usage by audience desirable to advertisers Ability to provide data about audience Organisations interested in the site's audience have money to spend on advertising Willingness of the community/ stakeholders to allow ads on the site	Sales function for ad space (or revenue share to ad network) Ad server (though some are available at no cost) Materials to communicate ad rates, demographics and ad sizes to potential advertisers	Direct ad sales can be time consuming Too little traffic to generate meaningful revenue stream Reducing user trust
Philanthropic funding	Can be from individuals, foundations, or government agencies Can be start-up investment in new project, unrestricted operating grants, or restricted to specific programmes	Project mission is aligned with mission of granting agencies/ individuals Ability to make a persuasive case that this project is the best use of resources towards advancing that mission	Development capacity Reporting on grants	Funding agency priorities change

(*Continued*)

Table 9.2 **Summary of revenue generation options (*cont'd*)**

Model	Description	Success factors	Costs	Risks
Content licensing	Granting one or more outside organisations permission and responsibility for distributing content Sharing in the revenue in the form of royalties	Content of interest to one or more distributors Ability to negotiate favourable licence terms	Legal costs	Limiting future options of what can be done with the content Channel conflict (if content is distributed through multiple channels)

Notes

1. Kevin Guthrie, Rebecca Griffiths and Nancy Maron. *Sustainability and Revenue Models for Online Academic Resources. An Ithaka Report.* May 2008. Online at: *http://www.ithaka.org/ithaka-s-r/strategy/sustainability-and-revenuemodels-for-online-academic-resources.*
2. 'Online academic resources' are defined as 'projects whose primary aim is to make content and scholarly discourse available on the web for research, collaboration, and teaching. This includes scholarly journals and monographs as well as a vast array of new formats that are emerging to disseminate scholarship, such as preprint servers and wikis. It also includes digital collections of primary source materials, datasets, and audio-visual materials that universities, libraries, museums, archives and other cultural and educational institutions are putting online.'
3. Adapted from European Commission. *EuropeAid Co-operation Office General Affairs Evaluation. Project Cycle Management Handbook. Version 2.0 March 2002.* Prepared by: PARTICIP GmbH, 2002.

10

Using information and communication technology in project management

Introduction

It is inconceivable now to think of any project manager in libraries, archives or museums operating without using some form of ICT. Most probably all project managers make frequent and regular use of the Microsoft (MS) Office suite (Word and Excel at a minimum), Macintosh or open source equivalents in all aspects of their work. Being a competent user of word processing, spreadsheet and database applications is a basic requirement for any project manager. There are now many other software applications with the potential to improve project management through the adoption and use of emerging technology applications providing, for instance, web 2.0 social networking functions and based on cloud computing.[1]

A printed book, however, is hardly the place for comprehensive coverage of ICT applications for project management; the speed of change and development of new features and functions in every version of an application precludes anything but the briefest coverage. For instance, as this book is being prepared for publication Microsoft is about to issue its MS Project 2010 and MS Outlook 2010, which will no doubt surpass their 2007 predecessors in size and functionality.

There are two approaches to using ICT in project management, not exclusive but dependent in large part upon the size and complexity of the project and the IT competence and know-how of the key players, including the project manager. The first is to adopt a whole project management solution and use a project management application with a range of different functions. The second is to take a more task-oriented approach and use specialist applications to address discrete tasks in project management; this may include, for instance, using MS Project only to do scheduling and critical path analysis without making use of its other features.

Table 10.1 suggests some of the key project management tasks that cut across several or all the main areas of project management and are undertaken more or less continuously in different project circumstances by the project manager and members of the project team.

This chapter is not intended as a comprehensive assessment of the current ICT market; it is intended to suggest some open source and proprietary applications that are worthy of consideration for both approaches, and to examine some of the issues and challenges that underpin the project manager's decisions about what ICT tools should be adopted by the project team.

Project management applications

There are many applications on the market that purport to offer a total project management solution. MS Project is the de facto industry standard and there will be many library, museum and archival organisations (or their parent bodies)

Table 10.1 Repeating tasks in project management areas

	Project planning and review	Managing partnerships	Managing risk	Managing resources	Monitoring and evaluation	Quality management
Problem solving	X		X			X
Scheduling	X			X		
Time and task management		X	X	X		
Costing and budgeting				X		
Project controls			X		X	X
Communication	X	X		X		

that have adopted MS Project either in its stand-alone or server version. This does not necessarily mean, however, that single projects should adopt its use.

The application creates critical path schedules, which are visualised in a Gantt chart. MS Project can recognise different classes of users, who can have differing access levels to projects, views, and other data. Custom objects such as calendars, views, tables, filters and fields can be stored at organisational level and shared by all users. MS Project also creates budgets based on assignment work and resource rates. As the software operates as part of the Microsoft Office suite, the later versions also provide for cross-functionality with presentational applications like PowerPoint and Visio.

MS Project is a 'big beast' designed for enterprise and industry and with features to meet the needs of project management professionals, which can be a challenge to master for those project managers with other 'day jobs', but which must be understood in order to effectively use the product. It is also expensive.

There are now several open source alternatives to MS Project, which divide roughly into two categories: those that have a similar look and feel to MS Project, fundamentally based on work planning using critical path schedules and Gantt charts, though often with very much more limited functionality; and those that take a very different approach to project management based on newer technology and rather different customer needs. Some examples of each category are suggested below.

MS Project challengers

Serena Openproj

Serena Openproj[2] is intended as a complete replacement for MS Project and claims to do everything it can do. Project plans can be imported from and exported to MS Project. In terms of functionality, if an open source and free alternative to MS Project, with all its bells and whistles, is required, then this is probably the application to choose.

GanttProject

GanttProject[3] features Gantt charting for work planning and scheduling of tasks, and resource management using resource load charts. A PERT chart can apparently be generated from the Gantt chart though it does not support critical path analysis. Project plans can be imported from and exported to MS Project and spreadsheet applications. If all that is required is a scheduling tool, which can generate professional looking time schedules and work plans, and can be changed easily, then GanttProject would fit the bill.

Figure 10.1 Screen shot from Openproj

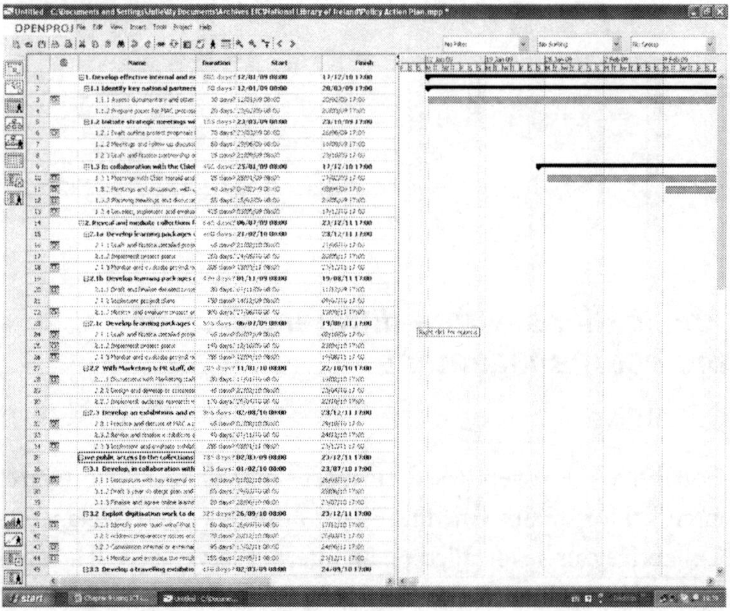

KPlato

KPlato[4] is basically a Gantt chart tool that can be used for work planning and scheduling. It is part of a larger KOffice suite but can be downloaded separately. It has a much simpler look and feel than most MS Project contenders while allowing project schedules to be reviewed and changed easily.

Figure 10.2 Screen shot of KPlato

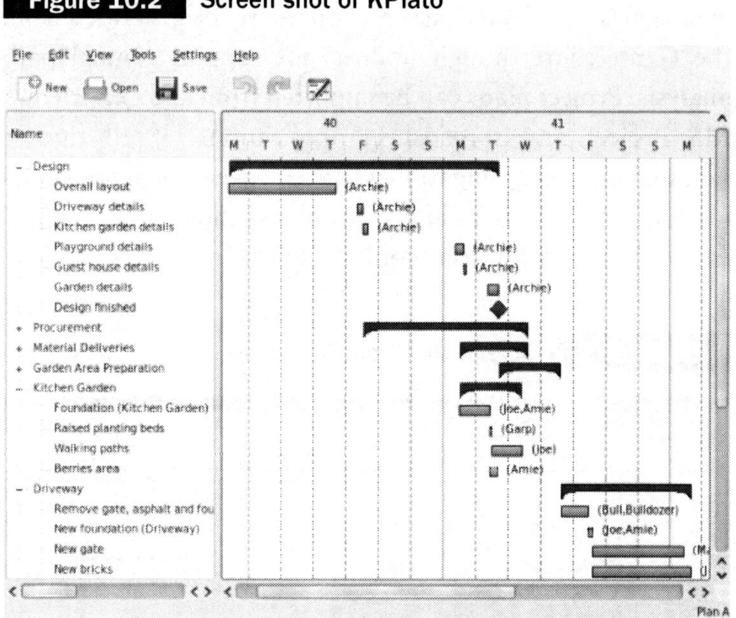

Applications with a different view of project management

Collabtive

Collabtive[5] is web-based project management software, intended for small to medium-sized businesses and freelancers. Collabtive can be installed on an internal server as well as used in the cloud. There are no Gantt chart or critical path features, but a set of simple desktop and more detailed views of project timescales, tasks, resources etc., very easy to use and to share.

Figure 10.3 Screen shot of Collabtive

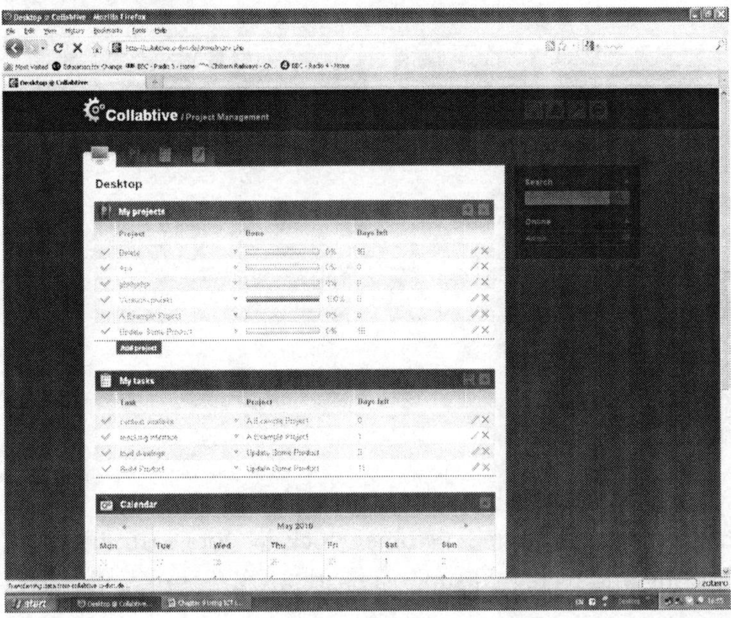

Project.net

Project.net[6] is a very interesting integration of social media tools such as wikis, blogs etc. with a complete project management application, which can be configured as a self-hosted in-house solution or a Project.net web-hosted solution. Project.net claims to be 'a complete Project Portfolio Management (PPM) solution . . . developed to resolve the major shortcoming of alternatives: weak adoption by teams, leading to minimal data entered into the system, resulting in a dearth of information for decision support at all levels.' While Project.net is an open source application available for free download from *sourceforge*[7] there are levels of modest

Figure 10.4 Screen shot of non-current version of Project.net from Wikipedia

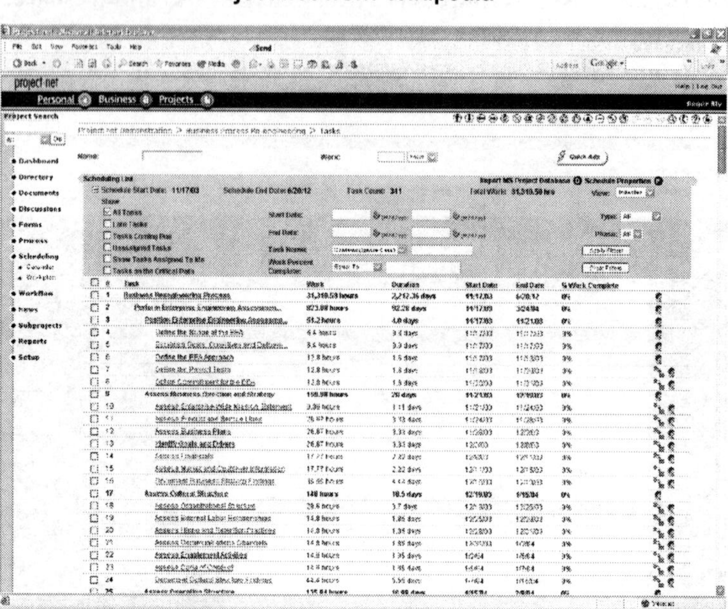

charging and some customer lock-in for customisation, hosting and technical support (with a UK base).

The task-oriented approach to choosing ICT tools

Aside from the complete project management solutions, project managers can choose to use a range of more specific proprietary or open source applications to address different tasks within project management.

Each of the key project management tasks shown in Table 10.1 can be greatly facilitated by the use of and competence in specific kinds of applications. In some areas, ICT has literally transformed project planning and implementation; for instance, in the power of spreadsheet applications to forecast and manipulate cost and other data and in the way that project teams can work across geographical boundaries.

The following are some suggestions of emerging and existing applications as exemplars of how ICT can be used to address different tasks.

Problem solving

SmartArt

Collaborative problem solving and planning can be greatly assisted by the visualisation of concepts and relationships between issues. If more than a flipchart and marker are needed then the 'SmartArt' features embedded into MS Word (MS Office 2007) provide a dynamic hierarchical chart facility (see 10.5).

Figure 10.5 **Screen shot of MS Office 2007 – MS Word and SmartArt**

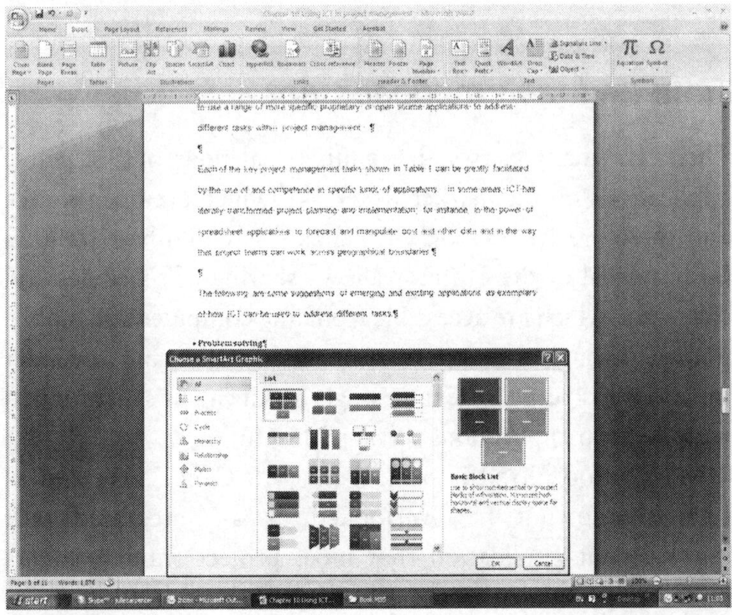

XMind

XMind[8] is an open source brainstorming and mind mapping software tool. It helps people to capture ideas, organise the ideas into various charts, and share them for collaboration. It supports mind maps, Ishikawa diagrams (also called fishbone diagrams or cause-and-effect diagrams; see Figure 4.2), tree diagrams, etc.

Project scheduling and work planning

For these tasks a combination of critical path and Gantt chart functionality is really required, unless the project is a very straightforward or simple one in which it is easy to work out dependencies, in which case an application such as GanttProject (see above) would be sufficient. Gantt charts can also be created using MS Excel and Word, though the end result looks less sophisticated and it is difficult to make changes to the resulting chart.

Time and task management

There are many personal organiser, calendar and schedule applications on the market, several of which are open source and therefore free. Google Calendar[9] is cloud-based and is fairly typical of the genre: it allows sharing of schedules and calendars, which are accessible from any computer and mobile phones through a mobile version; it has alert and reminder functions including by text message; and it can be synchronised with desktop applications such as MS Outlook.

MS Outlook itself is part of the MS Office suite and as such should not be overlooked as an integrated task management application that most project team members might be persuaded to use effectively. It is widely known as

Figure 10.6 MS Outlook email, task management and calendar management

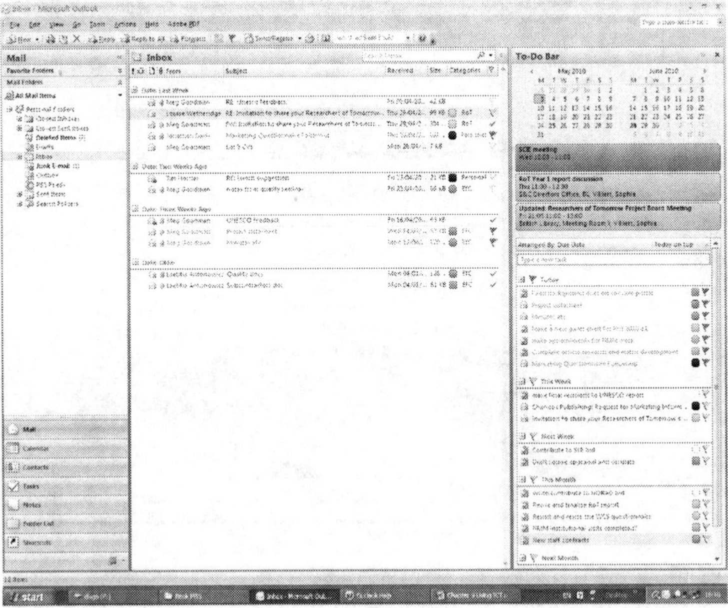

an e-mail application, though it includes contact management, a calendar and a task manager.

Costing and budgeting

Project managers, or someone on the project team, should be very competent spreadsheet software users. MS Excel or other equivalents, such as Open Office Calc[10] (Figure 10.7) are essential not only for budget planning and reviewing, but also for compiling and analysing much other monitoring data (for instance, usage levels for online services).

Project controls

Database software can be constructively used to set up common project and quality control databases and risk logs,

Figure 10.7 **Screen shot of Open Office Calc from Open office website**

Percent of Population of Age

	<15	15 – 65	65+
Asia	29	65	6
Europe	16	68	16
Africa	42	55	3
Australia and Oceania	25	65	10
North America	28	64	8
South America	29	65	6

using templates and reports to structure monitoring and control information. MS Access has advantages as it is part of the MS Office 2007 suite and therefore very commonly available. There are also several open source alternatives, which can be used as standalone applications or web-hosted (such as MySQL[11]). They all require, however, levels of ICT competence and know-how that may be beyond the capacity of the project team, and indeed unnecessary to the project's requirements. MS Access, as well as Excel and other spreadsheet applications, can be used with relatively limited skills to produce good and workable results (see the JISC infoNet Project Controls Database[12] as an example).

Communication

This is possibly the task area that has gained most from emerging technologies. Effective communication within projects – at all levels, within the project team, with stakeholders and beneficiaries, and among the partner organisations – is absolutely critical to project success. It could be said that the take-up of e-mail by organisations in the early 1990s made possible EU-funded multi-country research and development projects; emerging web 2.0 and other technologies now facilitate a whole range of organisational and individual communications, and which can be harnessed in projects to provide, for instance:

- *A project website:* a place and a space for project teams and stakeholders, as well as a window onto the project that can give access to project progress and messages intended for external funders, sponsors and the wider sector.
- *A stakeholder discussion forum:* embedded in the project website this can provide an important channel of communication on any critical project issues to which the project manager seeks input from, for instance, staff in project partner organisations other than project team members. These forums, however, need to be well managed and mediated if they are to be of real use, and this must be included in the calculation of project administration effort and costs.
- *Blogging and tweeting by staff:* this is almost certainly going to happen within project teams, with or without the project manager's intervention. The question will be how to stimulate and harness the use of blogs and Twitter to the project's best advantage.
- *Web conferences:* telephone and video conferencing is now a relatively trivial exercise using emerging technology solutions, and, perhaps, the most powerful of the communication tools at a project manager's disposal. Costs can be kept under control by reducing the need for face-to-face team meetings, while at the same time helping

to ensure cohesion among project teams (especially using web video). The use of Skype[13] software is widespread and allows users to make voice and webcam calls over the internet for free, as well as calling landline and mobile phones at greatly reduced costs. Skype also provides instant messaging and file transfer facilities.

Challenges for the project manager

In projects with multiple partner organisations the project manager can face a number of challenges, which will need careful consideration and investigation before ICT support for the project is chosen. Many of these potential challenges are associated with partner organisations using different ICT infrastructure and applications, such as:

- Institutional infrastructure and technical services cannot support the use of web-based or open source applications.
- Institutional network security policies and practices do not allow certain methods of, for instance, file transfer between partner and external organisations or providing remote but secure access to documents and files for all project team members and stakeholders from different organisations.

Since it is usually advisable that all project team members, from the start of the project, use the same applications for, in particular, time and task management, shared calendars and communication, the project manager must also take into account the varying levels of ICT skills and competencies among designated project team members, and staff willingness to learn quickly how to use new applications, or perhaps to change from using proprietary software to open source alternatives.

Notes

1. Cloud computing is essentially the management and provision of applications, information and data as a service provided over the Internet. It provides a convenient way of accessing computing services, independent of the hardware in use or physical location. It relieves the need to store information on computer or mobile devices with the assumption that the information can be quickly and easily accessed via the net. Google is one of the most prominent companies offering software as a free online service to billions of users across the world.
2. *http://www.serena.com/products/openproj/index.html*
3. *http://www.ganttproject.biz*
4. *http://www.koffice.org/kplato/*
5. *http://collabtive.o-dyn.de/*
6. *http://www.project.net/about*
7. *http://sourceforge.net/projects/projectnet/files/*
8. *http://www.xmind.net/*
9. *http://www.google.com/intl/en/googlecalendar/about.html*
10. *http://www.openoffice.org*
11. *http://dev.mysql.com/downloads/*
12. *http://www.jiscinfonet.ac.uk/infokits/projectmanagement/project-controls-database*
13. *http://www.skype.com/intl/en-gb/*

Useful resources

This section provides links to some sources of guidance, tools and resources additional to those drawn on and referenced in the text of this book.

Change management

learningforsustainability.net aims 'to provide a practical resource for those who work with communities (in the wider sense of the term) to help them identify and adopt more sustainable practices.' Of particular interest are the 'frameworks and tools for change' and those for 'evaluation and reflection': *http://learningforsustainability.net/.*

Monitoring and evaluation

Local Livelihoods target services to the 'international development and social economy sectors' and 'specialise in institutional strengthening and capacity building through providing training in the tools for programme and project management and monitoring and evaluation'. They publish the Results Based Monitoring & Evaluation Toolkit – Second edition 2009 by Freer Spreckley – available for free download at *http://www.uk.locallivelihoods.com/Moduls/WebSite/Page/Default.aspx?Pag_Id=109*

Monitoring and Evaluation News is a news service focusing on developments in monitoring and evaluation methods relevant to development programmes with social development objectives. The service can be accessed at *http://www.mande.co.uk*.

Project cycle management

Local Livelihoods target services to the 'international development and social economy sectors' and 'specialise in institutional strengthening and capacity building through providing training in the tools for programme and project management and monitoring and evaluation'. They publish the Project Cycle Management Toolkit (3rd edition 2009) by Freer Spreckley – free to download at *http://www.uk.locallivelihoods.com/Moduls/WebSite/Page/Default.aspx?Pag_Id=109*.

Project, programme or portfolio management

JISC infoNet is a UK advisory service for managers in the post-compulsory education sector promoting the effective strategic planning, implementation and management of information and learning technology. The service provides a free range of infoKits – *http://www.jiscinfonet.ac.uk/infokits* – on various planning and management issues including ones on Portfolio Management and Programme Management

The UK government, through the **Office of Government Commerce**, has invested heavily in programme management. The Office of Government Commerce has developed a methodology for programme management for public sector work in Europe; guidelines can be found at *http://www.ogc.gov.uk/ppm_resource_toolkit.asp*.

PRINCE2 is a process-based approach for project management, providing an easily tailored and scaleable project management methodology for the management of all types of projects. The method is the de facto standard for project management in the UK and is practised worldwide. PRINCE2 provides a range of free downloads and resources at *http://www.prince2.com/prince2-downloads.asp*.

The US **Project Management Institute** (PMI) offers project and programme management methodologies and guidelines for the private sector at *http://www.pmi.org/Pages/default.aspx*. PMI work underpins the PMBOK (see below).

The Project Management Body of Knowledge (PMBOK)

The Project Management Body of Knowledge (PMBOK) is a collection of processes and knowledge areas generally accepted as best practice within the project management discipline. As an internationally recognised standard (IEEE Standard 1490-2003: *http://standards.ieee.org/reading/ieee/std_public/description/se/1490-2003_desc.html*) it provides the fundamentals of project management, targeted at the construction, software, and engineering industries.

Project management software

For a very comprehensive list of available **project management software applications**, both proprietary and open source, see Wikipedia at *http://en.wikipedia.org/wiki/List_of_project_management_software*.

Glossary of project management terms

Accountability: Explaining decisions, actions or use of money to stakeholders.

Activities: The specific tasks to be undertaken during a project's life in order to obtain outputs.

Activity plan: A graphic representation, such as a Gantt chart, setting out the timing, sequence and duration of project activities. It can also be used to identify milestones for monitoring progress, and to assign responsibility for achievement of milestones.

Analysis of objectives: Checking that there is a clear means-to-end relationship between the objectives.

Appraisal: Analysis of a proposed project to determine its merit and acceptability in accordance with established criteria. This is the final step before a project is agreed for financing.

Assumptions: External factors which could affect the progress or success of the project, but over which the project manager has no direct control.

Baseline: Data used as a reference with which future results can be compared.

Beneficiary: Someone who benefits from the project outcomes; an end-user of project products or services.

Business case: The information that justifies the setting up, continuation or termination of the project. It answers the question 'Why should this project be done?' It is updated at key points throughout the project.

Contingency: An event that may occur but is not likely or intended.

Feasibility study: A feasibility study, conducted during the formulation stage, verifies whether the proposed project is well-founded, and is likely to meet the needs of its intended users. The study should design the project in full operational detail, taking account of all technical, economic, financial, institutional, management, environmental and social and cultural aspects.

Indicators: Indicators provide the basis for designing an appropriate monitoring system. Measurable indicators will show whether or not targets have been achieved to meet each objective.

Milestones: Milestones are points in the progress of a planned set of activities.

Monitoring: The systematic and continuous collection, analysis and use of information for the purpose of management control and decision-making.

Objectives: Description of how the aim of a project or programme is to be achieved. In its generic sense it refers to activities, outputs, project purpose, and overall outcome.

Project cycle: The project cycle follows the life of a project from the initial rationale through to its completion. It can provide a structure to ensure that stakeholders are consulted, and defines the key decisions, information requirements and responsibilities at each stage so that informed decisions can be made. It draws on evaluation to build experience from existing projects into the design of future programmes and projects.

Project cycle management: A methodology for the preparation, implementation and evaluation of projects and programmes.

Programme: A collection or portfolio of projects that together achieve a beneficial change for an organisation.

Stakeholder: Individuals or institutions with a financial or intellectual interest in the outputs of a project.

Sustainability: Sustainability is the ability to generate outputs after external support has been discontinued. While a project is limited by time, the benefits should continue and the activities should be developed long after the project has ended, without the need for external inputs. A key requirement for a successful project.

SWOT analysis: Analysis of an organisation's Strengths and Weaknesses, and the Opportunities and Threats that it faces. A tool used for project appraisal and review.

Terms of reference: Terms of reference define the tasks required, and indicate project background and objectives, planned activities, expected inputs and outputs, budget, timetables and job descriptions.

Transparency: Open communication and decision-making.

Variance: The difference between what was budgeted or planned and what is actually spent or done in a project.

Index

Lightning Source UK Ltd.
Milton Keynes UK
UKOW04f0449120914

238419UK00007B/76/P